PRACTICAL LEGAL ENGLISH

WRITING AS A U.S. LAWYER

■ ■ ■

Craig Hoffman, JD, PhD
Professor of U.S. Legal Discourse
Director, Legal English Program
Georgetown Law

WEST
ACADEMIC
PUBLISHING

444 Cedar Street, Suite 700
St. Paul, MN 55101
1-877-888-1330

Printed in the United States of America

ISBN: 978-1-68328-302-7

SUMMARY OF CONTENTS

TABLE OF CONTENTS

PRACTICAL LEGAL ENGLISH

WRITING AS A U.S. LAWYER

CHAPTER 1

WHAT IS LEGAL ENGLISH?

■ ■ ■

1. LEARNING LEGAL ENGLISH IS MORE THAN JUST LEARNING LEGAL VOCABULARY

When most non-U.S. lawyers think about U.S. Legal English, they tend to think about vocabulary and grammar. Somehow, they have been led to believe that memorizing legal terms and practicing grammar rules will make them better and more knowledgeable users of U.S. Legal English, and, consequently, better and more knowledgeable U.S. lawyers.

When many new U.S. law students think about U.S. legal writing, they too tend to think about vocabulary and grammar. They also seem to believe that memorizing legal terms and complicated legal phrases will make them better and more knowledgeable legal writers and, consequently, better and more knowledgeable lawyers.

Both of these groups, however, are ignoring the importance of background information and context when learning how to communicate about the law in the U.S. Much more is involved in becoming a fluent user of Legal English than just vocabulary and grammar.

2. LEGAL CONTEXT AND LEGAL MEANING

Individual words or individual sentences cannot be interpreted without understanding the contexts in which they are used. For example, the sentence in (1) can have (at least) two meanings in general English.

(1) John gave Mary no consideration.

In a non-legal context, Sentence (1) could mean that John ignored Mary or that he did not, in some relevant way, consider her qualifications—for example, for a job. It would mean something like Sentence (2).

(2) John did not consider Mary.

In a legal context, Sentence (1) could mean something entirely different. Depending on the context, it could have one of the general English meanings described above. If, however, John and Mary were involved in a contract dispute, John might argue that a contract does not exist between them because John had given nothing of value to Mary—that is, he gave Mary no legal consideration. In U.S. Legal English, *consideration* is a requirement in order for the parties to have a valid contract. Each party must give the other something of value; that thing is referred to as *consideration*.

Given this background, Sentence (1) is the most precise way to convey this meaning. Even though Sentence (1) and Sentence (2) can mean the same thing in general English, Sentence (2) cannot "mean" the same as Sentence (1) in Legal English.

In some sense, this simple example shows that one important difference between Legal English and general English appears to be as simple as knowing the particular definition of *consideration* in Legal English. Given just this type of example, you might agree with those who say mastering Legal English is no more than learning a few specialized terms. However, as we will see in our next example, there is much more involved in learning Legal English than simply learning legal vocabulary.

3. USING LEGAL SOURCES TO SUPPORT LEGAL CONCLUSIONS

Of course, in order to write a legal analysis of a legal problem in Legal English, you must know more than just proper general English grammar and vocabulary. You must also know how to fulfill a U.S. legal reader's expectations about what a proper U.S. legal analysis looks like. That is, you must know both English and Legal English. Knowing Legal English requires you to understand how U.S. lawyers think about U.S. law. Knowledge about the structure of the U.S. Legal System is essential background information in order to communicate effectively in Legal English.

A. ANALYZING A STATUTORY PROBLEM FOR A CLIENT

Let's consider the following example. Assume that Maria is a lawyer at a Spanish law firm in Madrid. She has been studying English for many years. In fact, the lawyers at her firm think that she is an excellent associate at the firm, and they have arranged to send Maria to the U.S. to the State of New Columbia[1] to work in a U.S. law firm. Maria has never studied U.S. law. Nevertheless, her spoken and written English are quite

[1] For this example, we refer to "New Columbia" rather than to an actual U.S. state. All states have their own bribery statutes and case law interpreting those statutes. The point of this example is to demonstrate discourse features of legal texts; it is not intended to be lesson about any state's bribery laws. Assume that New Columbia has a statutory code and a court system that includes New Columbia Trial Courts, New Columbia Appellate Courts, and a New Columbia Supreme Court.

good, so she feels quite confident that she can perform well in her new job at the U.S. law firm.

For her first assignment, Maria's supervisor tells her about one of the firm's clients, Senator Roger Stone, who is a member of the New Columbia State Senate. Senator Stone has been accused of accepting a bribe in a government "sting" operation. That is, a government agent, posing as a corrupt lobbyist for a pharmaceutical company, offered Senator Stone $1 million in a conversation regarding an upcoming vote in the state senate on a law that would favor the pharmaceutical industry. Senator Stone accepted the $1 million. He has now been charged with a violation of Code Section 11.56.110. As a defense, however, Senator Stone contends that he had always planned to vote in favor of the legislation. Therefore, he was not actually "bribed." The money was simply a gift.

i. Identifying the Relevant Statutory Law

Maria has been asked to write a memorandum evaluating whether a New Columbia court would be likely to accept Senator Stone's proposed defense. The relevant statute from the Criminal Code of the State of New Columbia appears below in (3).

> (3) **Code Section 11.56.110—Receiving a Bribe**
>
> (a) A public servant commits the crime of receiving a bribe if the public servant
>
> > (1) solicits a benefit with the intent that the public servant's vote, opinion, judgment, action, decision, or exercise of discretion as a public servant will be influenced; or
> >
> > (2) accepts or agrees to accept a benefit upon an agreement or understanding that the public servant's vote, opinion, judgment, action, decision, or exercise of discretion as a public servant will be influenced.
>
> (b) Receiving a bribe is a class B felony.

This is Maria's first assignment as a lawyer in the U.S. Although she graduated from an excellent law school in her own country, and she has been practicing law for several years in a law firm in the capital city there, she never had the opportunity to study in the U.S., and she is unfamiliar with the expectations of the U.S. legal reader. In writing her memorandum, she simply relies on her understanding of her own law and the expectations of legal readers in her home country. She writes a short memorandum for the lawyer who gave her the assignment. The analysis includes the following paragraph:

> (4) Section 11.56.110 of the New Columbia bribery statute **calls it a crime** for a public official to agree to "accept a benefit upon an agreement or understanding that the public servant's vote . . . will be influenced." Scholars

> who have recently written about this **code** agree that the government **should prove** that the public official actually changed his vote in response to the offer of a benefit. For example, Professor John Smith of Georgetown University Law Center, who is the world authority on "crimes of language" has analyzed the development of U.S. bribery law. He has determined that **"a benefit that is offered after the public official has made up his mind about an issue cannot be considered to be a bribe. Bribery requires a specific *quid pro quo.*"** Because our client did not change his vote in response to the benefit offered, he **will not be guilty** of bribery under the statute.

In many ways, this short paragraph might seem perfectly adequate to you. It identifies and quotes the relevant statute; it refers to an expert who precisely addresses the issue in the case; and it makes a specific conclusion about the client's situation. I have highlighted some features of Maria's text that would immediately alert a U.S. reader that she is not a native speaker of English. In addition, some of the phrases that Maria used would also signal that she is not familiar with U.S. Legal English.

For example, the phrase "calls it a crime" is not correct usage as a matter of general English. In English, we say that legislatures "make" certain acts a crime, rather than "calling" those acts a crime. Also, as a matter of Legal English, when U.S. lawyers refer to a specific code section, they say "statute" and not "code." The word code usually refers to an entire body of related statutory law; for example, the Criminal Code of New Columbia. Each code provision is referred to as a statute.

Notice, too, that the quote attributed to Professor Smith is not cited; that is, the writer has not told the reader where he could find the quoted language. Citation is very important because it tells the reader that the writer has legal authority to support his arguments. Further, the phrases "should prove" and "will not be guilty" represent improper uses of modal verbs. When discussing what a state is required to show in order to prove that someone has committed a crime, lawyers would probably use the modal "must." This indicates that if the state does not prove this, it will lose the case. The modal "should" is not appropriate here.

In the next example of highlighted language, a U.S. lawyer would probably not use the verb phrase, "will not be guilty," in this context. The lawyer here is trying to predict what a court would do in our case. A lawyer can never be 100 percent sure of what a court would do. In this case, the lawyer would probably say "it is **unlikely** that a court would. . ." Because a court's ruling could depend on many other factors, the lawyer would "hedge" a bit on the conclusion.

The examples that I have discussed for possible changes to Maria's paragraph fall under the categories of both general English and Legal

English. Making the suggested changes, the paragraph, now in (5), appears to be better.

> (5) Section 11.56.110 of the New Columbia bribery statute **makes it a crime** for a public official to agree to "accept a benefit upon an agreement or understanding that the public servant's vote . . . will be influenced." Scholars who have recently written about this **statute** agree that the government **must prove** that the public official actually changed his vote in response to the offer of a benefit. For example, Professor John Smith of Georgetown University Law Center, who is the world authority on bribery law, has analyzed the development of U.S. bribery law. He has determined that "a benefit that is offered after the public official has made up his mind about an issue cannot be considered to be a bribe. Bribery requires a specific *quid pro quo*."[2] Because our client did not change his vote in response to the benefit offered, **a court is unlikely to find our client guilty** of bribery under the statute.

ii. Using Case Law to Support a Statutory Analysis of the Client's Problem

Unfortunately for Maria, the legal analysis in her memorandum will not meet the expectations of her supervisor—who is a U.S. lawyer. Even though the English and Legal English "errors" have been corrected, the paragraph would still not be considered adequate to a U.S. lawyer. It lacks important features of legal analysis that would be obvious to a U.S. legal reader.

In this course, you will learn to evaluate several types of legal texts as you participate in the representation of a client. Although you will certainly improve your mastery of general English as you proceed through this semester, you will also improve your mastery and awareness of Legal English.

Compare Maria's analysis in (5) to the one in (6). The analysis in (6) is much better as a matter of Legal English because the writer has structured the analysis in a way that satisfies the expectations of a U.S. legal reader. As you read the analysis in (6), try to identify how it differs from Maria's analysis.

---

[2] John Smith. The Law of Bribery. Georgetown University Press (2005).

(6) It is unlikely that our client will be found guilty of receiving a bribe under New Columbia law. 11 New Columbia Statutes 11.56.110 (2003). The statute requires the accused to have accepted a benefit "upon agreement or understanding that the public servant's vote . . . will be influenced."[3] The New Columbia Supreme Court has recently ruled that a public official who has made up his mind about a vote cannot "be influenced" to vote the same way. *State v. Jones,* 232 New Columbia Reporter 364 (2005). In *State v. Jones*, the court considered a public official who had made several statements to the press that he was determined to vote in favor of specific legislation that benefited the tobacco industry. The state later prosecuted him for accepting lavish presents, including sports cars and exotic vacations, from representatives of a major tobacco company. The court concluded that this activity did not constitute a "bribe" under the statute because there was no evidence that the gifts from the tobacco industry had in fact caused him to change his vote on the legislation. *State v. Jones* at 366. In *State v. Brown*, however, the

In Legal English, the reader needs to know right away what the writer's legal conclusion is. The writer states what his legal conclusion is and then uses the analysis to explain why he thinks the relevant legal sources support this conclusion.

Next, the writer has quoted the relevant portion of the statute that governs the analysis. The entire statute appears in Footnote 3. The reader can then see the statutory context of the quoted language.

After quoting the relevant statutory language, the writer must then explain how the relevant courts have interpreted it in similar circumstances to the client's case.

Here, the writer must tell the reader the legally significant facts from this case so that the reader can understand how the court applied the statute to these facts. Notice, the writer does not tell the reader ALL of the facts of the case, but only those facts that will help the reader to understand the court's reasoning on the specific legal point being discussed.

---

[3] **New Columbia Statute: Receiving a Bribe**

(a) A public servant commits the crime of receiving a bribe if the public servant

(1) solicits a benefit with the intent that the public servant's vote, opinion, judgment, action, decision, or exercise of discretion as a public servant will be influenced; or

(2) accepts or agrees to accept a benefit upon an agreement or understanding that the public servant's vote, opinion, judgment, action, decision, or exercise of discretion as a public servant will be influenced.

(3) Receiving a bribe is a class B felony.

New Columbia Court of Appeals ruled that a public official who changed his vote after receiving a benefit from a lobbyist had "received a bribe" under New Columbia 11.56.110. *State v. Brown*, 229 New Columbia Appeals Reporter 782 (2006). Our client seems to be in the same position as the defendant in *State v. Jones*. Because our client did intend to vote in favor of the pharmaceutical bill before the benefit was offered to him, it is unlikely that a New Columbia court will find him guilty of a bribe.

> Here, the writer explains that there are other cases where courts have found a violation of the statute. The writer is telling the reader that the crucial fact in this case is that the public official changed his voting preference after he received the gifts. By explaining these two cases, the writer has demonstrated what the courts have found to be the legally significant facts in bribery cases under this statute.

> Here, the writer restates the legal conclusion which began this section of his legal analysis. Now, however, the reader understands what other courts have done in similar contexts. In Legal English, the reader always wants to understand how the writer uses case law to support his legal conclusions. First, the reader wants to see the legal conclusion; then he wants to see how the writer arrived at that conclusion by analyzing precedent; and then he wants to see the legal conclusion again, incorporating that analysis into the legal conclusion.
>
> This structure is the foundation of all legal writing in the US.

The New Columbia Supreme Court has also ruled that it is the burden of the state to show that the public official changed his vote in response to the benefit offered. *State v. White*, 214 New Columbia Reporter 23 (2001). Because the defendant in *State v. Jones* had made public statements prior to the alleged bribe, it was difficult for the government to meet its burden to show that the defendant had changed his vote because of the benefit offered. Although no evidence of prior statements exists in our case, it is the government that must prove that our client changed his vote in response to the promise of the benefit. *See State v. Black*, 223 New Columbia Reporter 859 (2002) (holding that the government bears a high burden of proving a causal relationship between a vote by a public official and the promise of a benefit).

> Here, the writer is alerting the reader to another relevant part of this law. The burden of proof is always an important aspect of a legal analysis. The writer here simply states the rule from *State v. White*. The writer then explains how the court in *State v. Jones* applied this rule in that case. Finally, the writer makes a legal conclusion about the client's case and cites *State v. Black* to support the conclusion that it is unlikely that the client will be found guilty under the statute. Although this legal argument is somewhat convincing, it would be made stronger if the writer had provided a discussion of more cases. As a legal reader, I want to know more about what courts have considered to be enough evidence to meet the burden of proof under the statute.

As you read cases and create legal arguments in this class, you will be using both English and Legal English—both are important. The goal of this class is for you to increase your awareness about your use of English and Legal English so that you can confidently create legal arguments in the documents that you write. Whether you are writing a legal memorandum in a law firm context or answering questions on a law school exam or a state bar exam, you will use both your English and Legal English skills.

B. ANALYZING A COMMON LAW PROBLEM FOR A CLIENT

In the U.S., many legal problems are addressed by purely common law legal analyses. That is, for many legal conflicts, the only relevant law is found in the court cases of the jurisdiction: there is no relevant statutory law. For cases like this, the legal writer must research the case law in the relevant jurisdiction and try to predict what a court would do in the client's case, based on what courts have done in other similar cases.

Having learned some of the lessons of Legal English in her first assignment, Maria is eager to meet the challenge of her next assignment: the analysis of a purely common law legal problem in the U.S. Assume that Maria has just interviewed a client who wants to bring a lawsuit in New Columbia state court for damages that he received when he was attacked by his neighbor's pet. These lawsuits are quite common under state common law in the U.S. The facts of the case appear below:

> *The client, Mr. Smith, was visiting his friend, Mr. Jones at Mr. Jones's home. Mr. Jones owns a pet that he calls Max. Max is a "poodle-wolf." That is, Max is a mixed-breed pet: he is one half French poodle and one half North American Gray Wolf. On most occasions, Max is very well-behaved. He lives in Mr. Jones's apartment; he plays with pet toys; and he eats pet food from a bowl. Although, Max is a large animal, and he looks quite dangerous, he has not attacked anyone since he has been living with Mr. Jones.*
>
> *On this day, however, when Mr. Smith tried to pet Max, Max jumped on him, pushed him to the ground, and caused Mr. Smith to break his right arm. Mr. Jones was quite surprised at Max's behavior and apologized to Mr. Smith. Nonetheless, Mr. Smith would like to file a lawsuit against Mr. Jones for negligence under the common law of New Columbia. Mr. Smith would like to allege that Mr. Jones was negligent by not warning him about Max's vicious propensities and that his not warning Mr. Smith was the proximate cause of his injuries.*

i. Identifying the Relevant Common Law

Maria needs to do some research. Because there is no New Columbia statute that governs this type of negligence action, she must read cases from New Columbia courts that have addressed similar fact situations. After several hours of searching for cases in the New Columbia database on Westlaw and writing summaries of relevant cases for herself, she has identified the following eight New Columbia cases:

Applicable New Columbia Negligence Cases

***Gerber v. Mills*, 632 A.2d 128 (N.C. 2012).**

A pet will qualify as a "dog," and its owner will be protected by the "one free bite" rule if the pet is a "domestic animal" by parentage, and the pet "behaves like a dog." This case establishes this two-prong test and clarifying the "one free bite" standard.

***Jones v. Stevens*, 545 A.2d 237 (N.C. 1986).**

Under New Columbia law, every dog gets "one free bite." In this case, the court decided that the owner of the pet was not liable for the injuries to the plaintiff because the owner had no evidence that his pet had vicious propensities. Courts will only hold pet owners liable who know, or should know, that their pets have behaved aggressively in the past. This rule is intended to protect pet owners from litigation; it derives from a general public policy in this state to encourage pet ownership. Only owners who know, or should know, that their pets have vicious propensities will have a duty to protect the public from their actions.

***Simon v. Brown*, 345 A.2d 542 (N.C. 1969).**

Ownership of domestic pets, especially dogs and cats, is central to good citizenship in New Columbia.

***State v. Snodgrass*, 460 A.2d 362 (N.C. 1980).**

A red fox that lived in its owner's house and drank apple juice from a baby bottle was considered to be a domesticated animal under the state leash law.

***Starr v. Reno*, 612 A.2d 693 (N.C. 2010).**

In cases of mixed origin, in order for a pet to be a domestic animal, the pet's parentage must be at least one half from a domestic breed.

***Stockton v. Meyers*, 421 A.2d 345 (N.C. 1975).**

The court allowed protection to the owner of a pet that was half coyote and half mixed-breed dog because the pet lived in its owner's apartment and drank milk from a bowl and, therefore, "behaved like a dog" for the purposes of the rule.

***Stone v. Broadbent*, 463 A.2d 24 (N.C. 2013).**

Owners of a half-wolf animal were not accorded the protection of the "one free bite" rule. Because their pet roamed free on their farm, ate wild birds, and mixed socially with full-blooded wolves, the owner should have known that it might have had vicious propensities because it did not "behave like a dog" for the purposes of the rule.

***Tower v. Busch*, 456 A.2d 243 (N.C. 1977).**

French poodle is a domestic breed—despite its name.

ii. Using Case Law to Support a Common Law Analysis of the Client's Problem

As we observed in the last legal problem involving the New Columbia bribery statute, the legal reader wants to know what the legal issue is and wants the legal writer to predict what a New Columbia court is likely to decide on the facts of this client's specific case. More important than that, her supervisor, who is a U.S. the legal reader, expects that Maria will explain how a New Columbia court is likely to apply the law to the facts of this case based on what it has done in other similar cases.

After thinking about the cases for a while, Maria has decided that a New Columbia court would probably not award damages to her client, Mr. Smith, in this case. Maria's supervisor at the firm has asked Maria to submit her analysis of New Columbia law to him. Maria sends him the following legal discussion:

Legal Analysis

Applicable Law

In *Gerber v. Mills*, 632 A.2d 128 (N.C. 2012), the court ruled that a pet will qualify as a "dog," and its owner will be protected by the "one free bite" rule if 1) the pet is a "domestic animal" by parentage; and 2) the pet "behaves like a dog." This case establishes this two-prong test and clarifying the "one free bite" standard. In cases of mixed origin, in order for a pet to be a domestic animal, the pet's parentage must be at least one half from a domestic breed. *Starr v. Reno*, 612 A.2d 693 (N.C. 2010). In *Tower v. Busch*, 456 A.2d 243 (N.C. 1977), the court ruled that French poodle is a domestic breed—despite its name.

In *Stockton v. Meyers,* 421 A.2d 345 (N.C. 1975), the court allowed protection to the owner of a pet that was half coyote and half mixed-breed dog because the pet lived in its owner's apartment and drank milk from a bowl and, therefore, "behaved like a dog" for the purposes of the rule. In *Stone v. Broadbent*, 463 A.2d 24 (N.C. 2013), however, owners of a half-wolf animal were not been accorded the protection of the "one free bite" rule. Because their pet roamed free on their farm, ate wild birds, and mixed socially with full-blooded wolves, it did not "behave like a dog" for the purposes of the rule.

Legal Conclusion

Because the defendant's pet in this case is one half French poodle, and because it behaves like a dog, the defendant will be protected by the "one free bite" rule.

Maria is very proud of her analysis. She believes that she has learned a lot from her experience writing the analysis of the New Columbia bribery statute. Here, she has presented descriptions of the relevant law from the New Columbia courts. At the end of her analysis, she has stated her conclusion, based on her reading of the case law.

Unfortunately, this discussion of the law is not at all satisfying to her supervisor. Although Maria has identified the relevant law and stated a reasonable legal conclusion, she has not specifically explained how a court would apply that law to the facts of her client's case.

Maria is an excellent lawyer. She just has not spent enough time in the U.S. learning about common law legal analysis. Her supervisor has asked her to get some help from another associate at the firm, Juan Carlos, who is also from Spain. Juan Carlos took a U.S. Legal Research, Writing, and Analysis class as part of his LLM at Georgetown Law. Maria explained the facts of the case to Juan Carlos (in English) and showed Juan Carlos her legal research on the relevant law in New Columbia.

Juan Carlos then wrote the Legal Analysis, which appears below. I have made comments on the Legal Analysis to point out what Juan Carlos has done:

Legal Analysis

1. The Pet Owner Must Be on Notice That His Pet Has Vicious Propensities

In order for a pet owner to be liable for any damages attributable to the actions of his pet, the owner must be "on notice" that his pet has "vicious propensities." The courts have consistently ruled that a pet owner must have some knowledge that his pet is likely to cause injury before the courts will impose a duty on him to protect the public from the actions of his pet. However, once a pet owner knows, or should know based on his pet's behavior, that the pet could be dangerous, he has a duty to protect others from the pet's actions. Stated differently, under New Columbia law, every dog gets "one free bite." *See Jones v. Stevens*, 545 A.2d 237 (N.C. 1986). This rule is intended

> Here, the writer has given some background about the applicable law. He states it in a way that will help the reader to understand how a court might apply the law in the client's case.

to protect pet owners from unwanted litigation; it derives from a general public policy in this state to encourage pet ownership. *Simon v. Brown*, 345 A.2d 542 (N.C. 1969) (declaring that ownership of domestic pets, especially dogs and cats, is central to good citizenship in New Columbia).

2. The New Columbia Courts Have Developed a Two-Part Test

The New Columbia courts have developed a two-part test to determine whether a pet owner will be entitled to protection under this one free bite rule. *Gerber v. Mills*, 632 A.2d 128 (N.C. 2012) (setting forth this two-part test and clarifying the "one free bite" standard). Defendant's pet will qualify as a "dog," and defendant will be protected by the "one free bite" rule because: a) defendant's poodle-wolf is a "domestic animal" by parentage; and b) defendant's poodle-wolf "behaves like a dog."

> Here, the writer explicitly applies the law to the facts of the client's case. This "roadmap" sets up the following discussion of the law as it relates specifically to the client's case.

a. The Pet Must Be One Half Domestic Breed by Parentage

In cases of mixed origin such as the client's case, in order for a pet to be a domestic animal, the pet's parentage must be at least one half from a domestic breed. *Starr v. Reno*, 612 A.2d 693 (N.C. 2010). In *Starr*, the pet was one a breed that was primarily cocker spaniel, but a small part Arizona cayote. The court accepted a report from a veterinarian that established the parentage of the pet. Because defendant's pet is one half French poodle, and French poodle is a domestic breed, defendant's pet is a domestic animal by parentage. *Tower v. Busch*, 456 A.2d 243 (N.C. 1977) (holding that French poodle is a domestic breed—despite its name). The defendant would most likely have to submit a report to the court establishing the parentage of his pet to satisfy this part of the *Starr* test.

> Again, the writer here has stated the rule and given a citation to a case where it was applied. He then applies the rule to the client's case. Sections a. and b. follow the same order as in the roadmap paragraph.

b. The Pet Must Behave Like a Dog

Whether a court will decide that the defendant's poodle-wolf behaves like a dog is a factual inquiry. The owner of a pet that was half coyote and half mixed-breed dog was accorded the protection of the "one free bite rule" because the pet lived in its owner's apartment and drank milk from a bowl and, therefore, "behaved like a dog" for the purposes of the rule. *Stockton v. Meyers*, 421 A.2d 345 (1975). Because the rule is intended to encourage responsible pet ownership, protection is denied to owners of pets that do not engage in pet-like behavior. Because defendant's poodle-wolf lives with him at home, plays with pet toys and does tricks, it is likely that a court would find that it engages in pet-like behavior and, therefore, "behaves like a dog" for the purposes of the "one free bite" rule.

> Here, the writer begins this paragraph with a statement about the client's case. The reader is now prepared to see how the writer will apply the law.

> Here, the writer explicitly applies the law to the facts of the client's case.

Courts have emphasized the importance of both parts of the *Gerber* test. For example, owners of a domestic animal by parentage that was one half wolf were not accorded the protection of the one free bite rule because their pet roamed free on their farm, ate wild birds, and mixed socially with full-blooded wolves. On these facts, the court determined that the pet did not "behave like a dog" for the purposes of the rule. *Stone v. Broadbent,* 463 A.2d 24 (N.C. 2013). The facts of the *Stone* case are very different from the facts of our client's case. The court decided that the pet owner in *Stone* should be aware that his pet is possibly dangerous. Comparing the facts of these cases, it is likely that a court would find that our client's pet behaved like a dog for the purposes of the one free bite rule.

> In this paragraph, the writer gives further guidance to the reader about how the courts apply the law in these cases. Again, it is important to help the reader to understand how the common law courts view and apply the law in prior cases.

Because the test set forth in *Gerber* is a two-part test, even though a pet may be considered a domestic animal for other state law purposes, its owner will not be protected by the "one bite rule" unless the pet is both a domestic animal by parentage and behaves like a dog. For example, a red fox that lived in its owner's house and drank apple juice from a baby bottle was considered to be a domesticated animal under the state leash law. *State v. Snodgrass*, 466 A.2d 362 (N.C. 1980). In that case, the court noted in *dicta* that its owner, however, would not be protected under the "one free bite rule" because the fox would not meet the "domestic parentage" part of the *Gerber* test.

This paragraph explains that, even though a pet may be treated as a domestic pet under other parts of the law, the two-part test in *Gerber* will still apply in negligence cases.

3. Mr. Jones Will Not Be Liable for Mr. Smith's Injuries

The courts of New Columbia want to encourage responsible pet ownership, and they have created the one free bite rule in order to protect pet owners from litigation. The courts have split the burden of proof. The burden of proof is on the pet owner to show that his pet is at least one-half domestic breed by parentage, but the burden is on the on the plaintiffs to show that the owner knew or should have known that the pet had vicious propensities. In our case, Max is at least one half French poodle, and Mr. Jones had no prior knowledge that Max had vicious propensities. Max seems to meet the common law standard for behaving like a dog. It is likely that a court would not find Mr. Jones liable for Mr. Smith's injuries in this case.

4. MEETING THE U.S. LEGAL READER'S EXPECTATIONS FOR A COMMON LAW ANALYSIS

In this Chapter, we have seen that the U.S. legal reader has very clear expectations about Legal English. Of course, grammar and vocabulary are very important; however, the U.S. legal reader also wants the U.S. legal writer to carefully explain how the applicable statutory law and case law apply to the specific facts of the client's case. It is not enough to simply present the applicable law to the reader and expect that the reader will do his own legal analysis.

In the next Chapters, we will look at more complicated legal problems than we have seen in this Chapter. In each case, we will focus on how the U.S. legal writer must not only present the applicable law but also how he must explain what the courts have done with that law in other contexts and, ultimately, how a court is likely to apply that law to the client's case.

Mastering grammar, vocabulary, and common law legal analysis are all essential to becoming fluent in Legal English.

APPENDIX TO CHAPTER 1

JUSTICE ROBERTS' INTRODUCTION TO THE U.S. SUPREME COURT OPINION, *NATIONAL FEDERATION OF BUSINESS V. SEBELIUS*, AND THE SYLLABUS FOR THE OPINION

■ ■ ■

In the opinion, *National Federation of Business v. Sebelius,* 567 U.S. 519 (2012), Chief Justice Roberts wrote the opinion for a divided U.S. Supreme Court. The Court had to decide whether the U.S. Congress has the Constitutional authority to require citizens of the U.S. to comply with certain requirements under the Affordable Care Act, commonly referred to as Obamacare.

The full text of the opinion is available on-line. You can find it using the official citation: *National Federation of Business v. Sebelius,* 567 U.S. 519 (2012). It is a very long and complicated opinion. Although I do not suggest that you read it now, it is an excellent example of a Supreme Court opinion, and you might want to read it later: on a long flight or on a beach when you have some time.

Even though I think that reading the entire opinion is not necessary in this context, I do believe that one part of this opinion is directly relevant to your understanding of the U.S. legal system. Before he fully addressed the legal issues before the Court in this important case, Justice Roberts wrote a brilliant introduction to the opinion, where he carefully explained the relationship between the federal government and the people of the U.S. under the U.S. Constitution. I have reproduced and edited Justice Robert's' introduction to the opinion in this Appendix. As you read this, think about how the separation of powers in the U.S. legal system compares to your own legal system. Throughout this book, we will be exploring our federal system of government and how it affects how U.S. lawyers make common law arguments to support their legal conclusions.

For most U.S. Supreme Court cases, the Court provides a summary of the Court's opinion, which is called the Syllabus. This Syllabus is not part of the opinion, and it cannot be cited as law. It is provided as a helpful summary of the case for readers. I have also reproduced and edited the Court's Syllabus of the opinion here. Perhaps it will entice you to read the Court's full opinion on your next international flight.

1. JUSTICE ROBERTS' INTRODUCTION TO *NATIONAL FEDERATION OF INDEPENDENT BUSINESS V. SEBELIUS*

Today we resolve constitutional challenges to two provisions of the Patient Protection and Affordable Care Act of 2010: the individual mandate, which requires individuals to purchase a health insurance policy providing a minimum level of coverage; and the Medicaid expansion, which gives funds to the States on the condition that they provide specified health care to all citizens whose income falls below a certain threshold. We do not consider whether the Act embodies sound policies. That judgment is entrusted to the Nation's elected leaders. We ask only whether Congress has the power under the Constitution to enact the challenged provisions.

In our federal system, the National Government possesses only limited powers; the States and the people retain the remainder. Nearly two centuries ago, Chief Justice Marshall observed that "the question respecting the extent of the powers actually granted" to the Federal Government " is perpetually arising, and will probably continue to arise, as long as our system shall exist." *McCulloch v. Maryland,* 4 Wheat. 316, 405, 4 L.Ed. 579 (1819). In this case we must again determine whether the Constitution grants Congress powers it now asserts, but which many States and individuals believe it does not possess. Resolving this controversy requires us to examine both the limits of the Government's power, and our own limited role in policing those boundaries.

The Federal Government "is acknowledged by all to be one of enumerated powers." *Ibid.* That is, rather than granting general authority to perform all the conceivable functions of government, the Constitution lists, or enumerates, the Federal Government's powers. Congress may, for example, "coin Money," "establish Post Offices," and "raise and support Armies." Art. I, § 8, cls. 5, 7, 12. The enumeration of powers is also a limitation of powers, because "[t]he enumeration presupposes something not enumerated." *Gibbons v. Ogden,* 9 Wheat. 1, 195, 6 L.Ed. 23 (1824). The Constitution's express conferral of some powers makes clear that it does not grant others. And the Federal Government "can exercise only the powers granted to it." *McCulloch, supra,* at 405.

Today, the restrictions on government power foremost in many Americans' minds are likely to be affirmative prohibitions, such as contained in the Bill of Rights. These affirmative prohibitions come into play, however, only where the Government possesses authority to act in the first place. If no enumerated power authorizes Congress to pass a certain law, that law may not be enacted, even if it would not violate any of the express prohibitions in the Bill of Rights or elsewhere in the Constitution.

Indeed, the Constitution did not initially include a Bill of Rights at least partly because the Framers felt the enumeration of powers sufficed to restrain the Government. As Alexander Hamilton put it, "the Constitution is itself, in every rational sense, and to every useful purpose, A BILL OF RIGHTS." The Federalist No. 84, p. 515 (C. Rossiter ed. 1961). And when the Bill of Rights was ratified, it made express what the enumeration of powers necessarily implied: "The powers not delegated to the United States by the Constitution . . . are reserved to the States respectively, or to the people." U.S. Const., Amdt. 10. The Federal Government has expanded dramatically over the past two centuries, but it still must show that a constitutional grant of power authorizes each of its actions. See, *e.g., United States v. Comstock,* 560 U.S. 126, 130 S.Ct. 1949, 176 L.Ed.2d 878 (2010).

The same does not apply to the States, because the Constitution is not the source of their power. The Constitution may restrict state governments—as it does, for example, by forbidding them to deny any person the equal protection of the laws. But where such prohibitions do not apply, state governments do not need constitutional authorization to act. The States thus can and do perform many of the vital functions of modern government—punishing street crime, running public schools, and zoning property for development, to name but a few—even though the Constitution's text does not authorize any government to do so. Our cases refer to this general power of governing, possessed by the States but not by the Federal Government, as the "police power." See, *e.g., United States v. Morrison,* 529 U.S. 598, 618–619, 120 S.Ct. 1740, 146 L.Ed.2d 658 (2000).

"State sovereignty is not just an end in itself: Rather, federalism secures to citizens the liberties that derive from the diffusion of sovereign power." *New York v. United States,* 505 U.S. 144, 181, 112 S.Ct. 2408, 120 L.Ed.2d 120 (1992) (internal quotation marks omitted). Because the police power is controlled by 50 different States instead of one national sovereign, the facets of governing that touch on citizens' daily lives are normally administered by smaller governments closer to the governed. The Framers thus ensured that powers which "in the ordinary course of affairs, concern the lives, liberties, and properties of the people" were held by governments more local and more accountable than a distant federal bureaucracy. The Federalist No. 45, at 293 (J. Madison). The independent power of the States also serves as a check on the power of the Federal Government: "By denying any one government complete jurisdiction over all the concerns of public life, federalism protects the liberty of the individual from arbitrary power." *Bond v. United States,* 564 U.S. 211, 222, 131 S.Ct. 2355, 2364, 180 L.Ed.2d 269 (2011).

This case concerns two powers that the Constitution does grant the Federal Government, but which must be read carefully to avoid creating a general federal authority akin to the police power. The Constitution authorizes Congress to "regulate Commerce with foreign Nations, and among the several States, and with the Indian Tribes." Art. I, § 8, cl. 3. Our precedents read that to mean that Congress may regulate "the channels of interstate commerce," "persons or things in interstate commerce," and "those activities that substantially affect interstate commerce." *Morrison, supra,* at 609, 120 S.Ct. 1740 (internal quotation marks omitted). The power over activities that substantially affect interstate commerce can be expansive. That power has been held to authorize federal regulation of such seemingly local matters as a farmer's decision to grow wheat for himself and his livestock, and a loan shark's extortionate collections from a neighborhood butcher shop. See *Wickard v. Filburn,* 317 U.S. 111, 63 S.Ct. 82, 87 L.Ed. 122 (1942); *Perez v. United States,* 402 U.S. 146, 91 S.Ct. 1357, 28 L.Ed.2d 686 (1971).

Congress may also "lay and collect Taxes, Duties, Imposts and Excises, to pay the Debts and provide for the common Defence and general Welfare of the United States." U.S. Const., Art. I, § 8, cl. 1. Put simply, Congress may tax and spend. This grant gives the Federal Government considerable influence even in areas where it cannot directly regulate. The Federal Government may enact a tax on an activity that it cannot authorize, forbid, or otherwise control. See, *e.g., License Tax Cases,* 5 Wall. 462, 471, 18 L.Ed. 497 (1867). And in exercising its spending power, Congress may offer funds to the States, and may condition those offers on compliance with specified conditions. See, *e.g., College Savings Bank v. Florida Prepaid Postsecondary Ed. Expense Bd.,* 527 U.S. 666, 686, 119 S.Ct. 2219, 144 L.Ed.2d 605 (1999). These offers may well induce the States to adopt policies that the Federal Government itself could not impose. See, *e.g., South Dakota v. Dole,* 483 U.S. 203, 205–206, 107 S.Ct. 2793, 97 L.Ed.2d 171 (1987) (conditioning federal highway funds on States raising their drinking age to 21).

The reach of the Federal Government's enumerated powers is broader still because the Constitution authorizes Congress to "make all Laws which shall be necessary and proper for carrying into Execution the foregoing Powers." Art. I, § 8, cl. 18. We have long read this provision to give Congress great latitude in exercising its powers: "Let the end be legitimate, let it be within the scope of the constitution, and all means which are appropriate, which are plainly adapted to that end, which are not prohibited, but consist with the letter and spirit of the constitution, are constitutional." *McCulloch,* 4 Wheat., at 421.

Our permissive reading of these powers is explained in part by a general reticence to invalidate the acts of the Nation's elected leaders. "Proper respect for a coordinate branch of the government" requires that we strike down an Act of Congress only if "the lack of constitutional authority to pass [the] act in question is clearly demonstrated." *United States v. Harris,* 106 U.S. 629, 635, 1 S.Ct. 601, 27 L.Ed. 290 (1883). Members of this Court are vested with the authority to interpret the law; we possess neither the expertise nor the prerogative to make policy judgments. Those decisions are entrusted to our Nation's elected leaders, who can be thrown out of office if the people disagree with them. It is not our job to protect the people from the consequences of their political choices.

Our deference in matters of policy cannot, however, become abdication in matters of law. "The powers of the legislature are defined and limited; and that those limits may not be mistaken, or forgotten, the constitution is written." *Marbury v. Madison,* 1 Cranch 137, 176, 2 L.Ed. 60 (1803). Our respect for Congress's policy judgments thus can never extend so far as to disavow restraints on federal power that the Constitution carefully constructed. "The peculiar circumstances of the moment may render a measure more or less wise, but cannot render it more or less constitutional." Chief Justice John Marshall, A Friend of the Constitution No. V, Alexandria Gazette, July 5, 1819, in John Marshall's Defense of *McCulloch v. Maryland* 190–191 (G. Gunther ed. 1969). And there can be no question that it is the responsibility of this Court to enforce the limits on federal power by striking down acts of Congress that transgress those limits. *Marbury v. Madison, supra,* at 175–176.

The questions before us must be considered against the background of these basic principles.

2. THE COURT'S SYLLABUS FOR *NATIONAL FEDERATION OF INDEPENDENT BUSINESS V. SEBELIUS*

Syllabus[1]

In 2010, Congress enacted the Patient Protection and Affordable Care Act in order to increase the number of Americans covered by health insurance and decrease the cost of health care. One key provision is the individual mandate, which requires most Americans to maintain "minimum essential" health insurance coverage. 26 U.S.C. § 5000A. For individuals who are not exempt, and who do not receive health insurance through an employer or government program, the means of satisfying the requirement is to purchase insurance from a private company. Beginning in 2014, those who do not comply with the mandate must make a "[s]hared responsibility payment" to the Federal Government. § 5000A(b)(1). The Act provides that this "penalty" will be paid to the Internal Revenue Service

[1] The syllabus constitutes no part of the opinion of the Court but has been prepared by the Reporter of Decisions for the convenience of the reader. See *United States v. Detroit Timber & Lumber Co.*, 200 U.S. 321, 337, 26 S.Ct. 282, 50 L.Ed. 499 (1906).

(IRS) with an individual's taxes, and "shall be assessed and collected in the same manner" as tax penalties. §§ 5000A(c), (g)(1).

Another key provision of the Act is the Medicaid expansion. The current Medicaid program offers federal funding to States to assist pregnant women, children, needy families, the blind, the elderly, and the disabled in obtaining medical care. 42 U.S.C. § 1396d(a). The Affordable Care Act expands the scope of the Medicaid program and increases the number of individuals the States must cover. For example, the Act requires state programs to provide Medicaid coverage by 2014 to adults with incomes up to 133 percent of the federal poverty level, whereas many States now cover adults with children only if their income is considerably lower, and do not cover childless adults at all. § 1396a(a)(10)(A)(i)(VIII). The Act increases federal funding to cover the States' costs in expanding Medicaid coverage. § 1396d(y)(1). But if a State does not comply with the Act's new coverage requirements, it may lose not only the federal funding for those requirements, but all of its federal Medicaid funds. § 1396c.

Twenty-six States, several individuals, and the National Federation of Independent Business brought suit in Federal District Court, challenging the constitutionality of the individual mandate and the Medicaid expansion. The Court of Appeals for the Eleventh Circuit upheld the Medicaid expansion as a valid exercise of Congress's spending power, but concluded that Congress lacked authority to enact the individual mandate. Finding the mandate severable from the Act's other provisions, the Eleventh Circuit left the rest of the Act intact.

Held: The judgment is affirmed in part and reversed in part.

648 F.3d 1235, affirmed in part and reversed in part.

1. Chief Justice ROBERTS delivered the opinion of the Court with respect to Part II, concluding that the Anti-Injunction Act does not bar this suit.

The Anti-Injunction Act provides that "no suit for the purpose of restraining the assessment or collection of any tax shall be maintained in any court by any person," 26 U.S.C. § 7421(a), so that those subject to a tax must first pay it and then sue for a refund. The present challenge seeks to restrain the collection of the shared responsibility payment from those who do not comply with the individual mandate. But Congress did not intend the payment to be treated as a "tax" for purposes of the Anti-Injunction Act. The Affordable Care Act describes the payment as a "penalty," not a "tax." That label cannot control whether the payment is a tax for purposes of the Constitution, but it does determine the application of the Anti-Injunction Act. The Anti-Injunction Act therefore does not bar this suit. Pp. 2582–2584.

2. Chief Justice ROBERTS concluded in Part III-A that the individual mandate is not a valid exercise of Congress's power under the Commerce Clause and the Necessary and Proper Clause. Pp. 2585–2593.

(a) The Constitution grants Congress the power to "*regulate* Commerce." Art. I, § 8, cl. 3 (emphasis added). The power to *regulate* commerce presupposes the existence of commercial activity to be regulated. This Court's precedent reflects this understanding: As expansive as this Court's cases construing the scope of the commerce power have been, they uniformly describe the power as reaching "activity." *E.g., United States v. Lopez,* 514 U.S. 549, 560, 115 S.Ct. 1624, 131 L.Ed.2d 626. The individual mandate, however, does not regulate existing commercial activity. It instead compels individuals to *become* active in commerce by purchasing a product, on the ground that their failure to do so affects interstate commerce.

Construing the Commerce Clause to permit Congress to regulate individuals precisely *because* they are doing nothing would open a new and potentially vast domain to congressional authority. Congress already possesses expansive power to regulate what people do. Upholding the Affordable Care Act under the Commerce Clause would give Congress the same license to regulate what people do not do. The Framers knew the difference between doing something and doing nothing. They gave Congress the power to *regulate* commerce, not to *compel* it. Ignoring that distinction would undermine the principle that the Federal Government is a government of limited and enumerated powers. The individual mandate thus cannot be sustained under Congress's power to "regulate Commerce." Pp. 2585–2591.

(b) Nor can the individual mandate be sustained under the Necessary and Proper Clause as an integral part of the Affordable Care Act's other reforms. Each of this Court's prior cases upholding laws under that Clause involved exercises of authority derivative of, and in service to, a granted power. *E.g., United States v. Comstock,* 560 U.S. 126, 130 S.Ct. 1949, 176 L.Ed.2d 878. The individual mandate, by contrast, vests Congress with the extraordinary ability to create the necessary predicate to the exercise of an enumerated power and draw within its regulatory scope those who would otherwise be outside of it. Even if the individual mandate is "necessary" to the Affordable Care Act's other reforms, such an expansion of federal power is not a "proper" means for making those reforms effective. Pp. 2591–2593.

3. Chief Justice ROBERTS concluded in Part III-B that the individual mandate must be construed as imposing a tax on those who do not have health insurance, if such a construction is reasonable.

The most straightforward reading of the individual mandate is that it commands individuals to purchase insurance. But, for the reasons explained, the Commerce Clause does not give Congress that power. It is therefore necessary to turn to the Government's alternative argument: that the mandate may be upheld as within Congress's power to "lay and collect Taxes." Art. I, § 8, cl. 1. In pressing its taxing power argument, the Government asks the Court to view the mandate as imposing a tax on those who do not buy that product. Because "every reasonable construction must be resorted to, in order to save a statute from unconstitutionality," *Hooper v. California,* 155 U.S. 648, 657, 15 S.Ct. 207, 39 L.Ed. 297, the question is whether it is "fairly possible" to interpret the mandate as imposing such a tax, *Crowell v. Benson,* 285 U.S. 22, 62, 52 S.Ct. 285, 76 L.Ed. 598. Pp. 2593–2594.

4. Chief Justice ROBERTS delivered the opinion of the Court with respect to Part III-C, concluding that the individual mandate may be upheld as within Congress's power under the Taxing Clause. Pp. 2594–2595.

(a) The Affordable Care Act describes the "[s]hared responsibility payment" as a "penalty," not a "tax." That label is fatal to the application of the Anti-Injunction Act. It does not, however, control whether an exaction is within Congress's power to tax. In answering that constitutional question, this Court follows a functional approach, " [d]isregarding the designation of the exaction, and viewing its substance and application." *United States v. Constantine,* 296 U.S. 287, 294, 56 S.Ct. 223, 80 L.Ed. 233. Pp. 2594–2596.

(b) Such an analysis suggests that the shared responsibility payment may for constitutional purposes be considered a tax. The payment is not so high that there is really no choice but to buy health insurance; the payment is not limited to willful violations, as penalties for unlawful acts often are; and the payment is collected solely by the IRS through the normal means of taxation. Cf. *Child Labor Tax Case (Bailey v. Drexel Furniture Co.),* 259 U.S. 20, 36–37, 42 S.Ct. 449, 66 L.Ed. 817. None of this is to say that payment is not intended to induce the purchase of health insurance. But the mandate need not be read to declare that failing to do so is unlawful. Neither the Affordable Care Act nor any other law attaches negative legal consequences to not buying health insurance, beyond requiring a payment to the IRS. And Congress's choice of language—stating that individuals "shall" obtain insurance or pay a "penalty"—does not require reading § 5000A as punishing unlawful conduct. It may also be read as imposing a tax on those who go without insurance. See *New York v. United States,* 505 U.S. 144, 169–174, 112 S.Ct. 2408, 120 L.Ed.2d 120. Pp. 2595–2598.

(c) Even if the mandate may reasonably be characterized as a tax, it must still comply with the Direct Tax Clause, which provides: "No Capitation, or other direct, Tax shall be laid, unless in Proportion to the Census or Enumeration herein before directed to be taken." Art. I, § 9, cl. 4. A tax on going without health insurance is not like a capitation or other direct tax under this Court's precedents. It therefore need not be apportioned so that each State pays in proportion to its population. Pp. 2598–2599.

5. Chief Justice ROBERTS, joined by Justice BREYER and Justice KAGAN, concluded in Part IV that the Medicaid expansion violates the Constitution by threatening States with the loss of their existing Medicaid funding if they decline to comply with the expansion. Pp. 2633–2640.

(a) The Spending Clause grants Congress the power "to pay the Debts and provide for the . . . general Welfare of the United States." Art. I, § 8, cl. 1. Congress may use this power to establish cooperative state-federal Spending Clause programs. The legitimacy of Spending Clause legislation, however, depends on whether a State voluntarily and knowingly accepts the terms of such programs. *Pennhurst State School and Hospital v. Halderman,* 451 U.S. 1, 17, 101 S.Ct. 1531, 67 L.Ed.2d 694. "[T]he Constitution simply does not give Congress the authority to require the States to regulate." *New York, supra,* at 178, 112 S.Ct. 2408, 120 L.Ed.2d 120. When Congress threatens to terminate other grants as a means of pressuring the States to accept a Spending Clause program, the legislation runs counter to this Nation's system of federalism. Cf. *South Dakota v. Dole,* 483 U.S. 203, 211, 107 S.Ct. 2793, 97 L.Ed.2d 171. Pp. 2633–2637.

(b) Section 1396c gives the Secretary of Health and Human Services the authority to penalize States that choose not to participate in the Medicaid expansion by taking away their existing Medicaid funding. 42 U.S.C. § 1396c. The threatened loss of over 10 percent of a State's overall budget is economic dragooning that leaves the States with no real option but to acquiesce in the Medicaid expansion. The Government claims that the expansion is properly viewed as only a modification of the existing program, and that this modification is permissible because Congress reserved the "right to alter, amend, or repeal any provision" of Medicaid. § 1304. But the expansion accomplishes a shift in kind, not merely degree. The original program was designed to cover medical services for particular categories of vulnerable individuals. Under the Affordable Care Act, Medicaid is transformed into a program to meet the health care needs of the entire nonelderly population with income below 133 percent of the poverty level. A State could hardly anticipate that Congress's reservation of the right to "alter" or "amend" the Medicaid program included the power to transform it so dramatically. The Medicaid expansion thus violates the Constitution by threatening States with the loss of their existing Medicaid funding if they decline to comply with the expansion. Pp. 2636–2639.

(c) The constitutional violation is fully remedied by precluding the Secretary from applying § 1396c to withdraw existing Medicaid funds for failure to comply with the requirements set out in the expansion. See § 1303. The other provisions of the Affordable Care Act are not affected.

Congress would have wanted the rest of the Act to stand, had it known that States would have a genuine choice whether to participate in the Medicaid expansion. Pp. 2638–2640.

6. Justice GINSBURG, joined by Justice SOTOMAYOR, is of the view that the Spending Clause does not preclude the Secretary from withholding Medicaid funds based on a State's refusal to comply with the expanded Medicaid program. But given the majority view, she agrees with THE CHIEF JUSTICE's conclusion in Part IV-B that the Medicaid Act's severability clause, 42 U.S.C. § 1303, determines the appropriate remedy. Because THE CHIEF JUSTICE finds the withholding—not the granting—of federal funds incompatible with the Spending Clause, Congress' extension of Medicaid remains available to any State that affirms its willingness to participate. Even absent § 1303's command, the Court would have no warrant to invalidate the funding offered by the Medicaid expansion, and surely no basis to tear down the Affordable Care Act in its entirety. When a court confronts an unconstitutional statute, its endeavor must be to conserve, not destroy, the legislation. See, *e.g., Ayotte v. Planned Parenthood of Northern New Eng.,* 546 U.S. 320, 328–330, 126 S.Ct. 961, 163 L.Ed.2d 812. Pp. 2641–2642.

ROBERTS, C.J., announced the judgment of the Court and delivered the opinion of the Court with respect to Parts I, II, and III-C, in which GINSBURG, BREYER, SOTOMAYOR, and KAGAN, JJ., joined; an opinion with respect to Part IV, in which BREYER and KAGAN, JJ., joined; and an opinion with respect to Parts III-A, III-B, and III-D. GINSBURG, J., filed an opinion concurring in part, concurring in the judgment in part, and dissenting in part, in which SOTOMAYOR, J., joined, and in which BREYER and KAGAN, JJ., joined as to Parts I, II, III, and IV. SCALIA, KENNEDY, THOMAS, and ALITO, JJ., filed a dissenting opinion. THOMAS, J., filed a dissenting opinion.

CHAPTER 2

WHAT IS A U.S. LEGAL OPINION?

■ ■ ■

1. INTRODUCTION

In Chapter 1, we observed how Maria and Juan Carlos looked at two fairly simple U.S. legal problems: the first one involved the interpretation of a New Columbia statute on bribery; the second one involved the synthesis and interpretation of the New Columbia common law about the duty of pet owners to protect people from the vicious propensities of their pets. In Chapters 3 and 4, we will be looking carefully at how U.S. legal writers predict how a judge is likely to apply the law, based on prior judicial opinions, to new (and more complicated) law.

In order to do this, a U.S. legal writer must read a lot of judicial opinions where courts have applied the law to similar fact situations. Reading judicial opinions (also called cases) is a skill that you must learn as part of Legal English. The judicial opinion is a very special kind of U.S. legal writing. Before we proceed to Chapters 3 and 4, let's spend some time focusing on what a judicial opinion is and how this type of U.S. legal writing is similar to and different from the type of U.S. legal writing that you will be doing as a U.S. law student or an associate at a U.S. law firm.

2. MEETING A LEGAL READER'S EXPECTATIONS IN A U.S. LEGAL OPINION

Judicial opinions are written by judges. Judges have a very specific role in the U.S. legal system, and this role is reflected in their writing. Judges have to decide cases. They do this based on a written record and sometimes on the basis of oral arguments and jury verdicts. Whatever input that the judge may have, and whatever court he might be writing for, the judge must write an opinion that both makes clear decisions on the issues in the case and explains the reasons for those decisions.

Different legal readers have different expectations for judicial opinions. The parties to the case, who may not be lawyers themselves, are primarily interested in the outcome of the case: did I win or lose? For these readers, the judge needs to say little more than: "Plaintiff wins. Trust me." The lawyers in the case have somewhat higher expectations. They are primarily interested whether the court was persuaded by their specific arguments: did the judge believe my version of the law or my opponent's?

Judges often can generally satisfy these somewhat self-interested expectations rather easily. Because the lawyers in the case are intimately familiar with the issues and the conflicting arguments in the case, the judge needs to simply "leave tracks" in the opinion that will make it clear to the lawyers whose interpretation of the controlling law won the day.

In fact, for routine cases, judges often write opinions that will satisfy only this narrow set of legal readers. For cases that involve issues that could potentially be interesting to a wider legal audience, however, the expectations are much higher. Unfortunately, judges are often not so sensitive to the expectations of the possibly huge number of other legal readers who might want to use the case as precedent when trying to determine how a court might handle a future case. These legal readers are very disappointed when judges issue opinions that do not offer well-supported decisions.

In our common law system, judges should always acknowledge and explain authoritative texts that are relevant to their decisions. For example, if a judge is trying to decide how a New York state commercial statute applies to a party's case, he should (at a minimum) explain how the highest court in New York, the Court of Appeals, has applied that statute in similar circumstances. A legal reader will want to know what that authoritative court has said—the New York Court of Appeals, of course, is the highest judicial authority about what a New York statute means. The U.S. legal reader expects that the judge will have read the relevant opinions. Beyond that, and much more important, the U.S. legal reader expects the judge to analyze those opinions in a way that not only decides the case before him but also provides a basis for deciding future cases.

For the judge, identifying the relevant law and deciding the issues in the case are only the first step. As a good U.S. legal writer, the judge should also provide an analysis of the law he cites. That is, it is equally important that the judge carefully decide how to "orchestrate" his synthesis of the existing relevant law. Again, the interested legal reader expects the judge to do more than to simply report what the prior law is. He cannot just state a conclusion and report what happened in prior cases. By doing merely that, he would be saying to the reader "Here's my answer; here are the cases I relied on. Please go figure out for yourself how I got there." Again, unfortunately, some judges do just that. A judge's opinion is more valuable to the legal community if the judge directs his opinion beyond the immediate audience of the parties and the lawyers involved in the case.

For example, in the interpretation of a New York statute or the analysis of a body of New York common law on a specific legal topic, it is certainly essential for the judge to provide an analysis of what the highest relevant court has said on the topic. However, he should also bring other authoritative voices into his text. For example, it might be interesting to see how lower courts in New York have applied the statute, and, equally, it might be interesting to see how New Jersey courts have applied a similar New Jersey statute or area of common law. Further, it could be that the federal courts in the Second Circuit, which includes New York, have had occasion to interpret this statute. If so, the opinions of the Second Circuit courts could be interesting to legal readers.

A judge might also investigate what legal scholars have said about this statute or similar statutes. Although scholarly writing is not authoritative in the same way that opinions of the highest relevant court are authoritative, scholars can offer useful insights into how courts might (or should) interpret law.

Sometimes a judge will be faced with a brand new statute—no prior court opinions are available. In that case, a judge might look into the legislative history of the statute, or he might investigate what social or political events triggered the passage of the statute. This information might also be relevant and interesting to legal readers about older statutes that have been widely interpreted by the courts.

Legal readers will be more likely to be satisfied by a judge's opinion when the judge is relying on a variety of authoritative sources, and his opinion is precise about why these sources support his legal analysis. The judge's job as a legal writer is to collect the most authoritative sources that he can and to explain as fully as he can why these sources support his legal conclusions. He must compose an arrangement of other legal (and sometimes non-legal) voices in a structure that the legal reader will find convincing.

3. THE STRUCTURE OF U.S. LEGAL OPINION: MAKING EFFECTIVE COMMON LAW ARGUMENTS

It is very important for you to begin to become familiar with the distinctive form of argumentation found in the U.S. Legal English: the common law argument. You've heard about the differences between civil law and common law legal systems and could no doubt offer solid definitions of the two. However, understanding the differences in how arguments are constructed in the two legal systems is a more complicated matter. Learning how to recognize common law argumentation in U.S. Legal English and produce it in your own writing is a central challenge for effectively navigating U.S. law school and communicating with U.S. lawyers.

All good legal arguments begin with a clear articulation of the facts of the case at hand and identification of the pertinent legal issues the case raises. This is true for both the common law and civil law legal systems. Many of the features of U.S. Legal English will probably feel very familiar to you. However, once the facts and issues are laid out, the argumentation begins to look rather different.

As you read U.S. legal cases, law review articles, and memorandums produced by U.S. lawyers, you'll observe that they refer extensively to prior legal cases. U.S. judges base their judgments on how they think that the facts and the rationale of prior cases applies in their case. That is, the judges are limited by precedent. Judges are not at liberty to make up whatever new law they want as they examine the facts of a case before them and determine the outcome. They are obligated to consider how the facts and issues of the case at hand compare to previous cases involving the same issues. This includes paying close attention to the reasoning the judges used as they decided the previous cases.

One of the unique aspects of a common law system is that the judge's rationale for applying law in a particular way to the particular set of facts in the case at hand is as much a part of the law as the actual ruling. An important responsibility a judge has in writing a legal opinion is to demonstrate how the thinking involved in the decision is linked to and grows out of previous legal decisions.

As U.S. lawyers and judges discuss prior cases and how they relate to the case at hand, their arguments usually include five components. As you evaluate common law arguments, you should always look for these components. We will be referring to these five components in this book as the Common Law Argument Guide. This Common Law Argument Guide can be used for several purposes. First, you can use it as you read cases. As you read a case, try to identify how the judge supports his legal conclusions by referring to prior cases. If the judge does this, his legal arguments will be persuasive to a wide audience of U.S. legal readers. Second, when you are doing your own legal reading for class, you can use the Common Law Argument Guide to structure your reading. In fact, many students have used the Common Law Argument Guide to help them to write case briefs for their law classes. Third, when you are doing your own legal research—either for a client in private practice or for a legal research and writing class in law school, you can use the Common Law Argument Guide to help you to evaluate the cases that you find in your research.

For the rest of this book we will be referring to this list of components in the Common Law Argument Guide. The elements appear below:

Common Law Argument Guide

Whenever you are reading U.S. common law legal arguments in any form of U.S. Legal English-cases; law review articles; legal memorandums, you must evaluate the writer's common law arguments. The writer should make it easy for you to see how his legal conclusions are supported by the legal sources that he discusses and cites. That is, you must evaluate whether the writer has given you enough information in order to determine whether his common law arguments are successful and convincing. As you read U.S. common law arguments, try to focus on the following things:

1) **Precedent.** Think about how the writer has chosen the statutes and cases that are being used to support his legal conclusions. Are they from the appropriate jurisdiction? Are they state law or are they federal law? Are the cases from the highest court in the jurisdiction or from a lower court?

2) **Analogy.** Think about how the writer has used the legally significant facts in the cases that are cited. Has he explained how the legally significant facts in these cases are either similar to or different from the facts of the case that the writer is discussing?

3) **Legal Issue(s).** Think about the primary legal issues that the writer is addressing. Are these legal issues the same as those in the cases that the writer is citing? How are they the same or different?

4) **Legal Reasoning.** Think about the rationale the courts used in deciding the cited cases that the writer is discussing; that is, has the writer explained how each court applied the law to the facts in each case?

5) **Legal Conclusions.** Think about the writer's legal conclusions on the points that he is addressing. Has the writer convinced you that his legal conclusions are supported by the applicable law?

Not all examples of common law argumentation will contain exactly these five components, and the five components will not necessarily appear in this order. Often the writer will intertwine two components in a single sentence. Sometimes the lawyer or judge may feel that the precedent is clear enough that he does not need to give a full account of the significant facts of the prior case. However, as someone new to U.S. Legal English, you will find it useful to keep these five components of common law argumentation in mind as you read cases, journal articles, and memos and as you write your own legal documents for an audience of U.S. lawyers. This Common Law Argument Guide is meant to be just a guide, not a rigid template that must always be mechanically followed.

4. ANALYZING THE ARGUMENTS IN A U.S. SUPREME COURT OPINION: *ERIE V. TOMPKINS*

One of the best ways to learn about common law legal arguments is to read how the experts make them. Let's look carefully how Justice Brandeis of the U.S. Supreme Court constructed his legal argument in the famous case of *Erie v. Tompkins.* You might be reading this case in one of your other classes; however, our focus here will be specifically on how Justice Brandeis tried to successfully fulfill his legal reader's expectations. Although Justice Brandeis clearly satisfies the expectations of his immediate audience—the parties and the lawyers representing them, he is very intentionally aiming his opinion at a much wider audience.

Erie v. Tompkins consists of three separate opinions: a majority; a concurrence, and a dissent. Each of these texts contains the basics of good legal writing. The writer of each opinion identifies and states a legal issue that he will address; he then makes a legal conclusion; he also chooses relevant legal authorities on which he will base explanations of his legal conclusions; and he develops a coherent story about the current case that relies on his analysis of the cited authorities. All good legal writing does this.

A. SPECIFIC GUIDELINES FOR READING *ERIE V. TOMPKINS*

Justice Brandeis's majority opinion is reproduced below. Please read it through once. As you read it, use the Common Law Argument Guide to pay attention to the sources that Justice Brandeis cites and how he uses them to support his conclusion. Specifically, as you read Justice Brandeis's majority opinion, try to answer the following questions:

1. What was the specific legal question that the Court was addressing?
2. What is the procedural history of the case; what did the lower courts do?
3. How does Justice Brandeis characterize the lower courts' findings?
4. Why did Justice Brandeis disagree with what the lower courts did?
5. What specific reasons did he give to support his decision?
6. What different types of legal sources of law did he cite?
7. Do you think that he made a correct decision?

In order to fully understand the *Erie* opinion (or any legal opinion), you might have to read it three or four times. Each time you read it, you should take notes as you read, and try to focus on the Common Law Argument Guide and specific questions in the Guidelines provided for this case. Each time you read it, you will be able to read it faster, and you will comprehend more.

As you read the majority opinion in *Erie v. Tompkins*, pay special attention to how the writer (Justice Brandeis) uses authorities to support his arguments. To help you, I have made comments in the margins of the case. Please consider these comments as you read.

B. *ERIE V. TOMPKINS*: THE MAJORITY OPINION[1]

ERIE V. TOMPKINS

304 U.S. 64 (1938)

MR. JUSTICE BRANDEIS delivered the opinion of the Court.

The question for decision is whether the oft-challenged doctrine of Swift v. Tyson shall now be disapproved.

> Here, the writer begins his opinion by stating the legal question. A legal reader is always interested to know what exact legal issue the writer is addressing.

Tompkins, a citizen of Pennsylvania, was injured on a dark night by a passing freight train of the Erie Railroad Company while walking along its right of way at Hughestown in that state. He claimed that the accident occurred through negligence in the operation, or maintenance, of the train; that he was rightfully on the premises as licensee because on a commonly used beaten footpath which ran for a short distance alongside the tracks; and that he was struck by something which looked like a door projecting from one of the moving cars. To enforce that claim he brought an action in the federal court for Southern New York, which had jurisdiction because the company is a corporation of that state. It denied liability; and the case was tried by a jury.

> The writer uses these first several paragraphs to explain the facts of the case. What is the writer's tone? What sorts of facts does the writer focus on?

> **Point About Grammar.** This use of the pronoun "It" is vague. Grammatically, this pronoun could refer to the company or to the court? It would have been better for the writer to use the full noun phrase, "the company," to avoid that vagueness.

[1] The footnotes in a legal opinion are very important. In the footnotes, the judge gives the citations to the legal sources that he relies on in his legal arguments. He also can use the footnotes to explain some of his arguments more fully than he does in the text. It is always important to read the footnotes. For your first reading of the case, I have deleted the footnotes so that you can focus on the text itself and the arguments in it. At the end of this Chapter, I added an appendix where you can find the majority opinion, the dissenting opinion, and the concurring opinion—including all of their footnotes. I suggest that you read all three of these opinions after you have read the majority opinion here.

The Erie insisted that its duty to Tompkins was no greater than that owed to a trespasser. It contended, among other things, that its duty to Tompkins, and hence its liability, should be determined in accordance with the Pennsylvania law; that under the law of Pennsylvania, as declared by its highest court, persons who use pathways along the railroad right of way—that is, a longitudinal pathway as distinguished from a crossing—are to be deemed trespassers; and that the railroad is not liable for injuries to undiscovered trespassers resulting from its negligence, unless it be wanton or willful. Tompkins denied that any such rule had been established by the decisions of the Pennsylvania courts; and contended that, since there was no statute of the state on the subject, the railroad's duty and liability is to be determined in federal courts as a matter of general law.

The trial judge refused to rule that the applicable law precluded recovery. The jury brought in a verdict of $30,000; and the judgment entered thereon was affirmed by the Circuit Court of Appeals, which held (2 Cir., 90 F.2d 603, 604), that it was unnecessary to consider whether the law of Pennsylvania was as contended, because the question was one not of local, but of general, law, and that 'upon questions of general law the federal courts are free, in absence of a local statute, to exercise their independent judgment as to what the law is; and it is well settled that the question of the responsibility of a railroad for injuries caused by its servants is one of general law. * * * Where the public has made open and notorious use of a railroad right of way for a long period of time and without objection, the company owes to persons on such permissive pathway a duty of care in the operation of its trains. * * * It is likewise generally recognized law that a jury may find that negligence exists toward a pedestrian using a permissive path on the railroad right of way if he is hit by some object projecting from the side of the train.'

The Erie had contended that application of the Pennsylvania rule was required, among other things, by section 34 of the Federal Judiciary Act of September 24, 1789, c. 20, 28 U.S.C. s 725, 28 U.S.C.A. 725, which provides: 'The laws of the several States, except where the Constitution, treaties, or statutes of the United States otherwise require or provide, shall be regarded as rules of decision in trials at common law, in the courts of the United States, in cases where they apply.'

Because of the importance of the question whether the federal court was free to disregard the alleged rule of the Pennsylvania common law, we granted certiorari. 302 U.S. 671, 58 S.Ct. 50, 82 L.Ed. 518.

> Here the writer changes his formulation of the legal question. What can you infer from this statement of the question?
>
> As you read the rest of this opinion, notice that the writer begins each part of his discussion with "First, Second, Third, and Fourth." Do you think that a reader would find that useful? How could the writer have prepared the reader for that organization?

First. Swift v. Tyson, 16 Pet. 1, 18, 10 L.Ed. 865, held that federal courts exercising jurisdiction on the ground of diversity of citizenship need not, in matters of general jurisprudence, apply the unwritten law of the state as declared by its highest court; that they are free to exercise an independent judgment as to what the common law of the state is—or should be; and that, as there stated by Mr. Justice Story, 'the true interpretation of the 34th section limited its application to state laws, strictly local, that is to say, to the positive statutes of the state, and the construction thereof adopted by the local tribunals, and to rights and titles to things having a permanent locality, such as the rights and titles to real estate, and other matters immovable and intra-territorial in their nature and character. It never has been supposed by us, that the section did apply, or was designed to apply, to questions of a more general nature, not at all dependent upon local statutes or local usages of a fixed and permanent operation, as, for example, to the construction of ordinary contracts or other written instruments, and especially to questions of general commercial law, where the state tribunals are called upon to perform the like functions as ourselves, that is, to ascertain, upon general reasoning and legal analogies, what is the true exposition of the contract or instrument, or what is the just rule furnished by the principles of commercial law to govern the case.'

> In these paragraphs of the opinion, the writer gives his version of the law as it has been applied up until this point. What types of sources does he cite? What is his tone?

The Court in applying the rule of section 34 to equity cases, in Mason v. United States, 260 U.S. 545, 559, 43 S.Ct. 200, 204, 67 L.Ed. 396, said:

'The statute, however, is merely declarative of the rule which would exist in the absence of the statute.' The federal courts assumed, in the broad field of 'general law,' the power to declare rules of decision which Congress was confessedly without power to enact as statutes. Doubt was repeatedly expressed as to the correctness of the construction given section 34, and as to the soundness of the rule which it introduced. But it was the more recent research of a competent scholar, who examined the original document, which established that the construction given to it by the Court was erroneous; and that the purpose of the section was merely to make certain that, in all matters except those in which some federal law is controlling, the federal courts exercising jurisdiction in diversity of citizenship cases would apply as their rules of decision the law of the state, unwritten as well as written.

> Now the writer alerts the reader that this view of the law has been widely criticized. How does he support that claim? What sources does he cite? What is his tone in this section? What words does the writer use that might imply that the Swift doctrine is flawed?

Criticism of the doctrine became widespread after the decision of Black & White Taxicab & Transfer Co. v. Brown & Yellow Taxicab & Transfer Co., 276 U.S. 518, 48 S.Ct. 404, 72 L.Ed. 681, 57 A.L.R. 426. There, Brown &Yellow, a Kentucky corporation owned by Kentuckians, and the Louisville & Nashville Railroad, also a Kentucky corporation, wished that the former should have the exclusive privilege of soliciting passenger and baggage transportation at the Bowling Green, Ky., Railroad station; and that the Black & White, a competing Kentucky corporation, should be prevented from interfering with that privilege. Knowing that such a contract would be void under the common law of Kentucky, it was arranged that the Brown & Yellow reincorporate under the law of Tennessee, and that the contract with the railroad should be executed there. The suit was then brought by the Tennessee corporation in the federal court for Western Kentucky to enjoin competition by the Black & White; an injunction issued by the District Court was sustained by the Court of Appeals; and this Court, citing many decisions in which the doctrine of Swift & Tyson had been applied, affirmed the decree.

Second. Experience in applying the doctrine of Swift v. Tyson, had revealed its defects, political and social; and the benefits expected to flow from the rule did not accrue. Persistence of state courts in their own opinions on questions of common law prevented uniformity; and the impossibility of discovering a satisfactory line of demarcation between the province of general law and that of local law developed a new well of uncertainties.

> Again, the writer has chosen words with decidedly negative connotations here to describe the Swift doctrine.

On the other hand, the mischievous results of the doctrine had become apparent. Diversity of citizenship jurisdiction was conferred in order to prevent apprehended discrimination in state courts against those not citizens of the state. Swift v. Tyson introduced grave discrimination by noncitizens against citizens. It made rights enjoyed under the unwritten 'general law' vary according to whether enforcement was sought in the state or in the federal court; and the privilege of selecting the court in which the right should be determined was conferred upon the noncitizen. Thus, the doctrine rendered impossible equal protection of the law. In attempting to promote uniformity of law throughout the United States, the doctrine had prevented uniformity in the administration of the law of the state.

> The writer's topic sentence in this paragraph continues to reinforce the message that the Swift Doctrine is flawed. In addition to citing authoritative texts, the writer is using particular language to advance his argument.

The discrimination resulting became in practice far-reaching. This resulted in part from the broad province accorded to the so-called 'general law' as to which federal courts exercised an independent judgment. In addition to questions of purely commercial law, 'general law' was held to include the obligations under contracts entered into and to be performed within the state, the extent to which a carrier operating within a state may stipulate for exemption from liability for his own negligence or that of his employee;

> This topic sentence is also quite negative about the doctrine. Do you find this word choice to be convincing?

> Evaluate the sources that the writer has cited here. Why has he chosen these sources? Why do you think a legal reader would be persuaded by these sources?

the liability for torts committed within the state upon persons resident or property located there, even where the question of liability depended upon the scope of a property right conferred by the state and the right to exemplary or punitive damages. Furthermore, state decisions construing local deeds, mineral conveyances and even devises of real estate, were disregarded.

In part the discrimination resulted from the wide range of persons held entitled to avail themselves of the federal rule by resort to the diversity of citizenship jurisdiction. Through this jurisdiction individual citizens willing to remove from their own state and become citizens of another might avail themselves of the federal rule. And, without even change of residence, a corporate citizen of the state could avail itself of the federal rule by reincorporating under the laws of another state, as was done in the Taxicab Case.

The injustice and confusion incident to the doctrine of Swift v. Tyson have been repeatedly urged as reasons for abolishing or limiting diversity of citizenship jurisdiction. Other legislative relief has been proposed. If only a question of statutory construction were involved, we should not be prepared to abandon a doctrine so widely applied throughout nearly a century. But the unconstitutionality of the course pursued has now been made clear, and compels us to do so.

> Again, this topic sentence brings an increasingly harsh tone to the writer's view of the Swift Doctrine. Do you find this to be effective?

Third. Except in matters governed by the Federal Constitution or by acts of Congress, the law to be applied in any case is the law of the state. And whether the law of the state shall be declared by its Legislature in a statute or by its highest court in a decision is not a matter of federal concern. There is no federal general common law. Congress has no power to declare substantive rules of common law applicable in a state whether they be local in their nature or 'general,' be they commercial law or a part of the law of torts.

> Here, the writer uses this topic sentence to clearly state his legal conclusion about the Swift Doctrine. Do you think that the previous discussion will have convinced the legal reader that the writer is correct?

And no clause in the Constitution purports to confer such a power upon the federal courts. As stated by Mr. Justice Field when protesting in Baltimore & Ohio R.R. Co. v. Baugh, 149 U.S. 368, 401, 13 S.Ct. 914, 927, 37 L.Ed. 772, against ignoring the Ohio common law of fellow-servant liability: I am aware that what has been termed the general law of the country—which is often little less than what the judge advancing the doctrine thinks at the time should be the general law on a particular subject—has been often advanced in judicial opinions of this court to control a conflicting law of a state. I admit that learned judges have fallen into the habit of repeating this doctrine as a convenient mode of brushing aside the law of a state in conflict with their views. And I confess that, moved and governed by the authority of the great names of those judges, I have, myself, in many instances, unhesitatingly and confidently, but I think now erroneously, repeated the same doctrine. But, notwithstanding the great names which may be cited in favor of the doctrine, and notwithstanding the frequency with which the doctrine has been reiterated, there stands, as a perpetual protest against its repetition, the constitution of the United States, which recognizes and preserves the autonomy and independence of the states,—independence in their legislative and independence in their judicial departments. Supervision over either the legislative or the judicial action of the states is in no case permissible except as to matters by the constitution specifically authorized or delegated to the United States. Any interference with either, except as thus permitted, is an invasion of the authority of the state, and, to that extent, a denial of its independence.'

The fallacy underlying the rule declared in Swift v. Tyson is made clear by Mr. Justice Holmes. The doctrine rests upon the assumption that there is 'a transcendental body of law outside of any particular State but obligatory within it unless and until changed by statute,' that federal courts have the power to use their judgment as to what the rules of common law are; and that in the federal courts 'the parties are entitled to an independent judgment on matters of general law':

> The writer here emphasizes that he is aligned with Justice Holmes. Often, writers bring in other authoritative voices to support their legal conclusions. As you read this passage of the opinion, try to decide whether the writer has laid a sufficient predicate for this argument.
>
> Would a legal reader demand more analysis? Or do you think that this level of analysis is sufficient for a legal opinion?

> 'But law in the sense in which courts speak of it today does not exist without some definite authority behind it. The common law so far as it is enforced in a State, whether called common law or not, is not the common law generally but the law of that State existing by the authority of that State without regard to what it may have been in England or anywhere else.
>
> * * *
>
> 'The authority and only authority is the State, and if that be so, the voice adopted by the State as its own (whether it be of its Legislature or of its Supreme Court) should utter the last word.'

Thus the doctrine of Swift v. Tyson is, as Mr. Justice Holmes said, 'an unconstitutional assumption of powers by the Courts of the United States which no lapse of time or respectable array of opinion should make us hesitate to correct.' In disapproving that doctrine we do not hold unconstitutional section 34 of the Federal Judiciary Act of 1789 or any other act of Congress. We merely declare that in applying the doctrine this Court and the lower courts have invaded rights which in our opinion are reserved by the Constitution to the several states.

Fourth. The defendant contended that by the common law of Pennsylvania as declared by its highest court in Falchetti v. Pennsylvania R. Co., 307 Pa. 203, 160 A. 859, the only duty owed to the plaintiff was to refrain from willful or wanton injury. The plaintiff denied that such is the Pennsylvania law. In support of their respective contentions the parties discussed and cited many decisions of the Supreme Court of the state. The Circuit Court of Appeals ruled that the question of liability is one of general law; and on that ground declined to decide the issue of state law. As we hold this was error, the judgment is reversed and the case remanded to it for further proceedings in conformity with our opinion.

Reversed.

C. STRUCTURE OF THE COMMON LAW ARGUMENTS IN *ERIE V. TOMPKINS*

Justice Brandeis is an excellent legal writer. As you were reading his opinion, I assume that you were able to identify his organization, given the comments in the margins and based on your own familiarity with how writers structure texts. Justice Brandeis chose to use explicit markers: First, Second; Third; Fourth. Explicit markers like this help the reader to get through a text. Each section, which began with a marker, also had a topic sentence that introduced the phase of the argument that Justice Brandeis was then setting forth. The subsequent paragraphs in each section also began with topic sentences that alert the reader to the subtopics that Justice Brandeis wanted the reader to think about. The markers and the topic sentences helped Justice Brandeis to lead the reader through his text.

The four initial sentences with their markers appear below.

First. Swift v. Tyson, 16 Pet. 1, 18, 10 L.Ed. 865, held that federal courts exercising jurisdiction on the ground of diversity of citizenship need not, in matters of general jurisprudence, apply the unwritten law of the state as declared by its highest court; that they are free to exercise an independent judgment as to what the common law of the state is—or should be; and that, as there stated by Mr. Justice Story, 'the true interpretation of the 34th section limited its application to state laws, strictly local, that is to say, to the positive statutes of the state, and the construction thereof adopted by the local tribunals, and to rights and titles to things having a permanent locality, such as the rights and titles to real estate, and other matters immovable and intra-territorial in their nature and character.

> Justice Brandeis decided to begin his opinion with a short history of the Swift doctrine. This choice allowed the Justice to shape the way that the reader would think about the doctrine. Throughout this section, Justice Brandeis uses this prominent part of the text—the beginning of the argument—to shape the reader's point of view.

Second. Experience in applying the doctrine of Swift v. Tyson, had revealed its defects, political and social; and the benefits expected to flow from the rule did not accrue.

> Having established the somewhat shaky history of the doctrine, Justice Brandeis shifts the reader's attention to the long line of other legal authorities who also believed that the doctrine was flawed.

Third. Except in matters governed by the Federal Constitution or by acts of Congress, the law to be applied in any case is the law of the state. And whether the law of the state shall be declared by its Legislature in a statute or by its highest court in a decision is not a matter of federal concern.

> Finally, in this last section about the doctrine, Justice Brandeis sets out his conclusion that the way that the Court had been applying the Federal Judiciary Act was unconstitutional.

Fourth. The defendant contended that by the common law of Pennsylvania as declared by its highest court in Falchetti v. Pennsylvania R. Co., 307 Pa. 203, 160 A. 859, the only duty owed to the plaintiff was to refrain from willful or wanton injury.

> This fourth section is simply part of the direction that the Court will give to the lower court that will re-hear the case. It is important, but it is a different point from the overriding point about the Swift Doctrine. Justice Brandeis has made the conscious decision to leave this discussion to the end.

5. CONCLUSIONS

Justice Brandeis had a very difficult writer's task in this opinion. He had to get votes on the Court to overturn a doctrine that the Court had been using for quite some time. Because the Court is reluctant to do that, Justice Brandeis made two important decisions about his writing: 1) he framed the legal question to be squarely about overruling the *Swift* Doctrine; and 2) he structured his discussion to anticipate his reader's skepticism about overruling it. By framing the legal issue as directly and simply as he did, he immediately focused the reader on the issue that he wanted them to consider. There are countless ways that he could have framed the legal issue. The clear and simple statement that he chose set up his entire legal discussion. He also chose to make the legal issue the first sentence of his opinion:

> The question for decision is whether the oft-challenged doctrine of *Swift v. Tyson* shall now be disapproved.

With this simple sentence, Justice Brandeis cleverly shaped the perceptions of his readers. He introduced the legal issue, and he referred to the doctrine as "oft-challenged." For the reader, the answer seems clear: "Of course we would want to disapprove an oft-challenged doctrine."

Justice Brandeis then structures his argument to anticipate the questions that a legal reader might have about overruling the oft-challenged doctrine. Again, Justice Brandeis's audience was much wider than the parties to the case and their lawyers. He first had to convince at least four of his fellow Justices to go along with him, and then he had to provide an argument that would satisfy the lower court judges who would be interpreting the Federal Judiciary Act in a post-*Erie* era. Beyond that, a U.S. Supreme Court Justice has to anticipate the views of legal academics and practicing lawyers who will be extremely critical readers of his opinion.

Keeping all of this in mind, Justice Brandeis, as all good legal writers, structured his opinion to anticipate and address his reader's expectations. After carefully framing the issue, he first gave a short history of the doctrine. He next pointed out that judges and scholars have attacked the doctrine, and he then put forth what he believed to be the best path going forward. This conceptual structure is not immediately obvious, but I think that you will agree that it was quite effective.

In the Appendix to this Chapter, I have reproduced the entire *Erie v. Tompkins* opinion: the Majority; the Dissent; and the Concurrence. Because this opinion is one of the most famous in all of U.S. law, I suggest that you take the time to read it in full. It includes very useful discussions about the stricture of the U.S. government and the relationship between the federal and the state courts. *Erie v. Tompkins* is one of the "Greatest Hits" of the U.S. Supreme Court.

APPENDIX TO CHAPTER 2

UNEDITED SUPREME COURT OPINION OF *ERIE V. TOMPKINS*

■ ■ ■

ERIE V. TOMPKINS

304 U.S. 64 (1938)

MR. JUSTICE BRANDEIS delivered the opinion of the Court.

The question for decision is whether the oft-challenged doctrine of Swift v. Tyson[1] shall now be disapproved.

Tompkins, a citizen of Pennsylvania, was injured on a dark night by a passing freight train of the Erie Railroad Company while walking along its right of way at Hughestown in that state. He claimed that the accident occurred through negligence in the operation, or maintenance, of the train; that he was rightfully on the premises as licensee because on a commonly used beaten footpath which ran for a short distance alongside the tracks; and that he was struck by something which looked like a door projecting from one of the moving cars. To enforce that claim he brought an action in the federal court for Southern New York, which had jurisdiction because the company is a corporation of that state. It denied liability; and the case was tried by a jury.

***70** The Erie insisted that its duty to Tompkins was no greater than that owed to a trespasser. It contended, among other things, that its duty to Tompkins, and hence its liability, should be determined in accordance with the Pennsylvania law; that under the law of Pennsylvania, as declared by its highest court, persons who use pathways along the railroad right of way—that is, a longitudinal pathway as distinguished from a crossing—

---

[1] 1842, 16 Pet. 1, 10 L.Ed. 865. Leading cases applying the doctrine are collected in Black & White Taxicab, etc., Co. v. Brown & Yellow Taxicab, etc., Co., 276 U.S. 518, 530, 531, 48 S.Ct. 404, 407, 408, 72 L.Ed. 681, 57 A.L.R. 426. Dissent from its application or extension was expressed as early as 1845 by Mr. Justice McKinley (and Mr. Chief Justice Taney) in Lane v. Vick, 3 How. 464, 477, 11 L.Ed. 681. Dissenting opinions were also written by Mr. Justice Daniel in Rowan v. Runnels, 5 How. 134, 140, 12 L.Ed. 85; by Mr. Justice Nelson in Williamson v. Berry, 8 How. 495, 550, 558, 12 L.Ed. 1170; by Mr. Justice Campbell in Pease v. Peck, 18 How. 595, 599, 600, 15 L.Ed. 518; and by Mr. Justice Miller in Gelpcke v. City of Dubuque, 1 Wall. 175, 207, 17 L.Ed. 520, and U.S. ex rel. Butz v. City of Muscatine, 8 Wall. 575, 585, 19 L.Ed. 490. Vigorous attack upon the entire doctrine was made by the Mr. Justice Field in Baltimore & Ohio R.R. Co. v. Baugh, 149 U.S. 368, 390, 13 S.Ct. 914, 37 L.Ed. 772, and by Mr. Justice Holmes in Kuhn v. Fairmont Coal Co., 215 U.S. 349, 370, 30 S.Ct. 140, 54 L.Ed. 228, and in the Taxicab Case, 276 U.S. 518, at page 532, 48 S.Ct. 404, 408, 72 L.Ed. 681, 57 A.L.R. 426.

are to be deemed trespassers; and that the railroad is not liable for injuries to undiscovered trespassers resulting from its negligence, unless it be wanton or willful. Tompkins denied that any such rule had been established by the decisions of the Pennsylvania courts; and contended that, since there was no statute of the state on the subject, the railroad's duty and liability is to be determined in federal courts as a matter of general law.

The trial judge refused to rule that the applicable law precluded recovery. The jury brought in a verdict of $30,000; and the judgment entered thereon was affirmed by the Circuit Court of Appeals, which held (2 Cir., 90 F.2d 603, 604), that it was unnecessary to consider whether the law of Pennsylvania was as contended, because the question was one not of local, but of general, law, and that 'upon questions of general law the federal courts are free, in absence of a local statute, to exercise their independent judgment as to what the law is; and it is well settled that the question of the responsibility of a railroad for injuries caused by its servants is one of general law. * * * Where the public has made open and notorious use of a railroad right of way for a long period of time and without objection, the company owes to persons on such permissive pathway a duty of care in the operation of its trains. * * * It is likewise generally recognized law that a jury may find that negligence exists toward a pedestrian using a permissive path on the railroad right of way if he is hit by some object projecting from the side of the train.'

***71** The Erie had contended that application of the Pennsylvania rule was required, among other things, by section 34 of the Federal Judiciary Act of September 24, 1789, c. 20, 28 U.S.C. s 725, 28 U.S.C.A. ****819** s 725, which provides: 'The laws of the several States, except where the Constitution, treaties, or statutes of the United States otherwise require or provide, shall be regarded as rules of decision in trials at common law, in the courts of the United States, in cases where they apply.'

Because of the importance of the question whether the federal court was free to disregard the alleged rule of the Pennsylvania common law, we granted certiorari. 302 U.S. 671, 58 S.Ct. 50, 82 L.Ed. 518.

First. Swift v. Tyson, 16 Pet. 1, 18, 10 L.Ed. 865, held that federal courts exercising jurisdiction on the ground of diversity of citizenship need not, in matters of general jurisprudence, apply the unwritten law of the state as declared by its highest court; that they are free to exercise an independent judgment as to what the common law of the state is—or should be; and that, as there stated by Mr. Justice Story, 'the true interpretation of the 34th section limited its application to state laws, strictly local, that is to say, to the positive statutes of the state, and the construction thereof adopted by the local tribunals, and to rights and titles to things having a permanent locality, such as the rights and titles to real estate, and other matters immovable and intra-territorial in their nature and character. It never has been supposed by us, that the section did apply, or was designed to apply, to questions of a more general nature, not at all dependent upon local statutes or local usages of a fixed and permanent operation, as, for example, to the construction of ordinary contracts or other written instruments, and especially to questions of general commercial law, where the state tribunals are called upon to perform the like functions as ourselves, that is, to ascertain, upon general reasoning and legal analogies, what is the true exposition of the contract or ***72** instrument, or what is the just rule furnished by the principles of commercial law to govern the case.'

The Court in applying the rule of section 34 to equity cases, in Mason v. United States, 260 U.S. 545, 559, 43 S.Ct. 200, 204, 67 L.Ed. 396, said: 'The statute, however, is merely declarative of the rule which would exist in the absence of the statute.'[2] The federal courts assumed, in the broad field of 'general law,' the power to declare rules of decision which Congress was confessedly without power to enact as statutes. Doubt was repeatedly expressed as to the correctness of the construction given section 34,[3] and as to the soundness of the rule which it introduced.[4] But it was the more recent research of a competent scholar, who examined the original document, which established that the construction given to it by the Court was erroneous; and that the purpose of the section was merely to make certain that, in all matters except those in which some federal law is controlling, ***73** the federal courts exercising jurisdiction in diversity of citizenship cases would apply as their rules of decision the law of the state, unwritten as well as written.[5]

Criticism of the doctrine became widespread after the decision of ****820** Black & White Taxicab & Transfer Co. v. Brown & Yellow Taxicab &

---

[2] In Hawkins v. Barney's Lessee, 5 Pet. 457, 464, 8 L.Ed. 190, it was stated that section 34 'has been uniformly held to be no more than a declaration of what the law would have been without it: to wit, that the lex loci must be the governing rule of private right, under whatever jurisdiction private right comes to be examined.' See, also, Bank of Hamilton v. Dudley's Lessee, 2 Pet. 492, 525, 7 L.Ed. 496. Compare Jackson v. Chew, 12 Wheat. 153, 162, 168, 6 L.Ed. 583; Livingston v. Moore, 7 Pet. 469, 542, 8 L.Ed. 751.

[3] Pepper, The Border Land of Federal and State Decisions (1889) 57; Gray, The Nature and Sources of Law (1909 ed.) ss 533, 534; Trickett, Non-Federal Law Administered in Federal Courts (1906) 40 Am.L.Rev. 819, 821–824.

[4] Street, Is There a General Commercial Law of the United States (1873) 21 Am.L.Reg. 473; Hornblower, Conflict between State and Federal Decisions (1880) 14 Am.L.Rev. 211; Meigs, Decisions of the Federal Courts on Questions of State Law (1882) 8 So.L.Rev. (n.s.) 452, (1911) 45 Am.L.Rev. 47; Heiskell, Conflict between Federal and State Decisions (1882) 16 Am.L.Rev. 743; Rand, Swift v. Tyson versus Gelpcke v. Dubuque (1895) 8 Harv.L.Rev. 328, 341–343; Mills, Should Federal Courts Ignore State Laws (1900) 34 Am.L.Rev. 51; Carpenter, Court Decisions and the Common Law (1917) 17 Col.L.Rev. 593, 602, 603.

[5] Charles Warren, New Light on the History of the Federal Judiciary Act of 1789 (1923) 37 Harv.L.Rev. 49, 51–52, 81–88, 108.

Transfer Co., 276 U.S. 518, 48 S.Ct. 404, 72 L.Ed. 681, 57 A.L.R. 426.[6] There, Brown &Yellow, a Kentucky corporation owned by Kentuckians, and the Louisville & Nashville Railroad, also a Kentucky corporation, wished that the former should have the exclusive privilege of soliciting passenger and baggage transportation at the Bowling Green, Ky., Railroad station; and that the Black & White, a competing Kentucky corporation, should be prevented from interfering with that privilege. Knowing that such a contract would be void under the common law of Kentucky, it was arranged that the Brown & Yellow reincorporate under the law of Tennessee, and that the contract with the railroad should be executed there. The suit was then brought by the Tennessee corporation in the federal court for Western Kentucky to enjoin competition by the Black & White; an injunction issued by the District Court ***74** was sustained by the Court of Appeals; and this Court, citing many decisions in which the doctrine of Swift & Tyson had been applied, affirmed the decree.

Second. Experience in applying the doctrine of Swift v. Tyson, had revealed its defects, political and social; and the benefits expected to flow from the rule did not accrue. Persistence of state courts in their own opinions on questions of common law prevented uniformity;[7] and the impossibility of discovering a satisfactory line of demarcation between the province of general law and that of local law developed a new well of uncertainties.[8]

On the other hand, the mischievous results of the doctrine had become apparent. Diversity of citizenship jurisdiction was conferred in order to prevent apprehended discrimination in state courts against those not citizens of the state. Swift v. Tyson introduced grave discrimination by

---

[6] Shelton, Concurrent Jurisdiction—Its Necessity and its Dangers (1928) 15 Va.L.Rev. 137; Frankfurter, Distribution of Judicial Power Between Federal and State Courts (1928) 13 Corn.L.Q. 499, 524–530; Johnson, State Law and the Federal Courts (1929) 17 Ky.L.J. 355; Fordham, The Federal Courts and the Construction of Uniform State Laws (1929) 7 N.C.L.Rev. 423; Dobie, Seven Implications of Swift v. Tyson (1930) 16 Va.L.Rev. 225; Dawson, Conflict of Decisions between State and Federal Courts in Kentucky, and the Remedy (1931) 20 Ky.L.J. 1; Campbell, Is Swift v. Tyson an Argument for or against Abolishing Diversity of Citizenship Jurisdiction (1932) 18 A.B.A.J. 809; Ball, Revision of Federal Diversity Jurisdiction (1933) 28 Ill.L.Rev. 356, 362–364; Fordham, Swift v. Tyson and the Construction of State Statutes (1935) 41 W.Va.L.Q. 131.

[7] Compare Mr. Justice Miller in Gelpcke v. City of Dubuque, 1 Wall. 175, 209, 17 L.Ed. 520. The conflicts listed in Holt, The Concurrent Jurisdiction of the Federal and State Courts (1888) 160 et seq. cover twenty-eight pages. See, also, Frankfurter, supra note 6, at 524–530; Dawson, supra note 6; Note, Aftermath of the Supreme Court's Stop, Look and Listen Rule (1930) 43 Harv.L.Rev. 926; cf. Yntema and Jaffin, Preliminary Analysis of Concurrent Jurisdiction (1931) 79 U. of Pa.L.Rev. 869, 881–886. Moreover, as pointed out by judge Augustus N. Hand in Cole v. Pennsylvania R. Co., D.C., 43 F.2d 953, 956, 957, 71 A.L.R. 1096, decisions of this Court on common-law questions are less likely than formerly to promote uniformity.

[8] Compare 2 Warren, The Supreme Court in United States History, Rev.Ed. 1935, 89: 'Probably no decision of the Court has ever given rise to more uncertainty as to legal rights; and though doubtless intended to promote uniformity in the operation of business transactions, its chief effect has been to render it difficult for business men to know in advance to what particular topic the Court would apply the doctrine. * * *' The Federal Digest through the 1937 volume, lists nearly 1,000 decisions involving the distinction between questions of general and of local law.

noncitizens against citizens. It made rights enjoyed under the unwritten 'general law' vary according to whether enforcement was sought in the state ***75** or in the federal court; and the privilege of selecting the court in which the right should be determined was conferred upon the noncitizen.[9] Thus, the doctrine rendered ****821** impossible equal protection of the law. In attempting to promote uniformity of law throughout the United States, the doctrine had prevented uniformity in the administration of the law of the state.

The discrimination resulting became in practice far-reaching. This resulted in part from the broad province accorded to the so-called 'general law' as to which federal courts exercised an independent judgment.[10] In addition to questions of purely commercial law, 'general law' was held to include the obligations under contracts entered into and to be performed within the state,[11] the extent to which a carrier operating within a state may stipulate for exemption from liability for his own negligence or that of his employee;[12] the liability for torts committed within the state upon persons resident or property located there, even where the question of liability ***76** depended upon the scope of a property right conferred by the state;[13] and the right to exemplary or punitive damages.[14] Furthermore,

[9] It was even possible for a nonresident plaintiff defeated on a point of law in the highest court of a State nevertheless to win out by taking a nonsuit and renewing the controversy in the federal court. Compare Gardner v. Michigan Cent. R.R. Co., 150 U.S. 349, 14 S.Ct. 140, 37 L.Ed. 1107; Harrison v. Foley, 8 Cir., 206 F. 57; Interstate Realty & Inv. Co. v. Bibb County, 5 Cir., 293 F. 721; see Mills, supra note 4, at 52.

[10] For a recent survey of the scope of the doctrine, see Sharp & Brennan, The Application of the Doctrine of Swift v. Tyson since 1900 (1929) 4 Ind.L.J. 367.

[11] Black & White Taxicab & Transfer Co. v. Brown & Yellow Taxicab & Transfer Co., 276 U.S. 518, 48 S.Ct. 404, 72 L.Ed. 681, 57 A.L.R. 426; Rowan v. Runnels, 5 How. 134, 139, 12 L.Ed. 85; Boyce v. Tabb, 18 Wall. 546, 548, 21 L.Ed. 757; Johnson v. Chas. D. Norton Co., 6 Cir., 159 F. 361; Keene Five Cent Sav. Bank v. Reid, 8 Cir., 123 F. 221.

[12] New York Railroad Co. v. Lockwood, 17 Wall. 357, 367, 368, 21 L.Ed. 627; Liverpool & G. W. Steam Co. v. Phenix Ins. Co., 129 U.S. 397, 443, 9 S.Ct. 469, 32 L.Ed. 788; Eells v. St. Louis, K. & N.W. Ry. Co., C.C.S.D.Iowa, 52 F. 903; Fowler v. Pennsylvania R.R. Co., 2 Cir., 229 F. 373.

[13] Chicago v. Robbins, 2 Black 418, 428, 17 L.Ed. 298. Compare Yates v. Milwaukee, 10 Wall. 497, 506, 507, 19 L.Ed. 984; Yeates v. Illinois Cent. Ry. Co., C.C.N.D. Ill., 137 F. 943; Curtis v. Cleveland, C.C. & St. L. Ry. Co., C.C.E.D.Ill., 140 F. 777. See, also, Hough v. Texas Railway Co., 100 U.S. 213, 226, 25 L.Ed. 612; Baltimore & Ohio R.R. Co. v. Baugh, 149 U.S. 368, 13 S.Ct. 914, 37 L.Ed. 772; Gardner v. Michigan Cent. R.R. Co., 150 U.S. 349, 358, 14 S.Ct. 140, 37 L.Ed. 1107; Beutler v. Grand Trunk Junction Ry. Co., 224 U.S. 85, 32 S.Ct. 402, 56 L.Ed. 679; Baltimore & Ohio R.R. Co. v. Goodman, 275 U.S. 66, 48 S.Ct. 24, 72 L.Ed. 167, 56 A.L.R. 645; Pokora v. Wabash Ry. Co., 292 U.S. 98, 54 S.Ct. 580, 78 L.Ed. 1149. 91 A.L.R. 1049; Cole v. Pennsylvania R.R. Co., D.C., 43 F.2d 953, 71 A.L.R. 1096.

[14] Lake Shore & M.S. Ry. Co. v. Prentice, 147 U.S. 101, 106, 13 S.Ct. 261, 37 L.Ed. 97; Norfolk & P. Traction Co. v. Miller, 4 Cir., 174 F. 607; Greene v. Keithley, 8 Cir., 86 F.2d 238, 239.

state decisions construing local deeds,[15] mineral conveyances,[16] and even devises of real estate,[17] were disregarded.[18]

In part the discrimination resulted from the wide range of persons held entitled to avail themselves of the federal rule by resort to the diversity of citizenship jurisdiction. Through this jurisdiction individual citizens willing to remove from their own state and become citizens of another might avail themselves of the federal rule.[19] ****822** And, without even change of residence, a corporate citizen of ***77** the state could avail itself of the federal rule by reincorporating under the laws of another state, as was done in the Taxicab Case.

The injustice and confusion incident to the doctrine of Swift v. Tyson have been repeatedly urged as reasons for abolishing or limiting diversity of citizenship jurisdiction.[20] Other legislative relief has been proposed.[21] If only a question of statutory construction were involved, we should not be prepared to abandon a doctrine so widely applied throughout nearly a century.[22] But the unconstitutionality ***78** of the course pursued has now been made clear, and compels us to do so.

---

[15] Foxcroft v. Mallet, 4 How. 353, 379, 11 L.Ed. 1008; Midland Valley Ry. Co. v. Sutter, 8 Cir., 28 F.2d 163; Midland Valley Ry. Co. v. Jarvis, 8 Cir., 29 F.2d 539, 61 A.L.R. 1064.

[16] Kuhn v. Fairmont Coal Co., 215 U.S. 349, 30 S.Ct. 140, 54 L.Ed. 228; Mid-Continent Petroleum Corporation v. Sauder, 10 Cir., 67 F.2d 9, 12, reversed on other grounds 292 U.S. 272, 54 S.Ct. 671, 78 L.Ed. 1255, 93 A.L.R. 454.

[17] Lane v. Vick, 3 How. 464, 476, 11 L.Ed. 681; Barber v. Pittsburg, F.W. & C. Ry. Co., 166 U.S. 83, 99, 100, 17 S.Ct. 488, 41 L.Ed. 925; Messinger v. Anderson, 6 Cir., 171 F. 785, 791, 792, reversed on other grounds 225 U.S. 436, 32 S.Ct. 739, 56 L.Ed. 1152; Knox & Lewis & Alwood, D.C.S.D.Ga., 228 F. 753.

[18] Compare, also, Williamson v. Berry, 8 How. 495, 12 L.Ed. 1170; Watson v. Tarpley, 18 How. 517, 15 L.Ed. 509; Gelpcke v. City of Dubuque, 1 Wall. 175, 17 L.Ed. 520.

[19] See Cheever v. Wilson, 9 Wall. 108, 123, 19 L.Ed. 604; Robertson v. Carson, 19 Wall. 94, 106, 107, 22 L.Ed. 178; Morris v. Gilmer, 129 U.S. 315, 328, 9 S.Ct. 289, 32 L.Ed. 690; Dickerman v. Northern Trust Co., 176 U.S. 181, 192, 20 S.Ct. 311, 44 L.Ed. 423; Williamson v. Osenton, 232 U.S. 619, 625, 34 S.Ct. 442, 58 L.Ed. 758.

[20] See, e.g., Hearings Before a Subcommittee of the Senate Committee on the Judiciary on S. 937, S. 939, and S. 3243, 72d Cong., 1st Sess. (1932) 6–8; Hearing Before the House Committee on the Judiciary on H.R. 10594, H.R. 4526, and H.R. 11508, 72d Cong., 1st Sess., ser. 12 (1932) 97–104; Sen.Rep.No. 530, 72d Cong., 1st Sess. (1932) 4–6; Collier, A Plea Against Jurisdiction Because of Diversity (1913) 76 Cent.L.J. 263, 264, 266; Frankfurter, supra note 6; Ball, supra, note 6; Warren, Corporations and Diversity of Citizenship (1933) 19 Va.L.Rev. 661, 686.

[21] Thus, bills which would abrogate the doctrine of Swift v. Tyson have been introduced. S. 4333, 70th Cong., 1st Sess.; S. 96, 71st Cong., 1st Sess.; H.R. 8094, 72d Cong., 1st Sess. See, also, Mills, supra, note 4, at 68, 69; Dobie, supra, note 6, at 241; Frankfurter, supra, note 6, at 530; Campbell, supra, note 6, at 811. State statutes on conflicting questions of 'general law' have also been suggested. See Heiskell, supra, note 4, at 760; Dawson, supra, note 6; Dobie, supra, note 6, at 241.

[22] The doctrine has not been without defenders. See Eliot, The Common Law of the Federal Courts (1902) 36 Am.L.Rev. 498, 523–525; A. B. Parker, The Common Law Jurisdiction of the United States Courts (1907) 17 Yale L.J. 1; Schofield, Swift v. Tyson: Uniformity of Judge-Made State Law in State and Federal Courts (1910) 4 Ill.L.Rev. 533; Brown, The Jurisdiction of the Federal Courts Based on Diversity of Citizenship (1929) 78 U. of Pa.L.Rev. 179, 189–191; J. J. Parker, The Federal Jurisdiction and Recent Attacks Upon It (1932) 18 A.B.A.J. 433, 438; Yntema, The Jurisdiction of the Federal Courts in Controversies Between Citizens of Different States

Third. Except in matters governed by the Federal Constitution or by acts of Congress, the law to be applied in any case is the law of the state. And whether the law of the state shall be declared by its Legislature in a statute or by its highest court in a decision is not a matter of federal concern. There is no federal general common law. Congress has no power to declare substantive rules of common law applicable in a state whether they be local in their nature or 'general,' be they commercial law or a part of the law of torts. And no clause in the Constitution purports to confer such a power upon the federal courts. As stated by Mr. Justice Field when protesting in Baltimore & Ohio R.R. Co. v. Baugh, 149 U.S. 368, 401, 13 S.Ct. 914, 927, 37 L.Ed. 772, against ignoring the Ohio common law of fellow-servant liability: I am aware that what has been termed the general law of the country—which is often little less than what the judge advancing the doctrine thinks at the time should be the general law on a particular subject—has been often advanced in judicial opinions of this court to control a conflicting law of a state. I admit that learned judges have fallen into the habit of repeating this doctrine as a convenient mode of brushing aside the law of a state in conflict with their views. And I confess that, moved and governed by the authority of the great names of those judges, I have, myself, in many instances, unhesitatingly and confidently, but I think now erroneously, repeated the same doctrine. But, notwithstanding the great names which may be cited in favor of the doctrine, and notwithstanding the frequency with which the doctrine has been reiterated, there stands, as a perpetual protest against its repetition, the constitution of the United States, which recognizes and preserves the autonomy and independence of the states,—independence in their legislative and independence ***79** in their judicial departments. Supervision over either the legislative or the judicial action of the states is in no case permissible except as ****823** to matters by the constitution specifically authorized or delegated to the United States. Any interference with either, except as thus permitted, is an invasion of the authority of the state, and, to that extent, a denial of its independence.'

The fallacy underlying the rule declared in Swift v. Tyson is made clear by Mr. Justice Holmes.[23] The doctrine rests upon the assumption that there is 'a transcendental body of law outside of any particular State but obligatory within it unless and until changed by statute,' that federal courts have the power to use their judgment as to what the rules of common law are; and that in the federal courts 'the parties are entitled to an independent judgment on matters of general law':

(1933) 19 A.B.A.J. 71, 74, 75; Beutel, Common Law Judicial Technique and the Law of Negotiable Instruments—Two Unfortunate Decisions (1934) 9 Tulane L.Rev. 64.

[23] Kuhn v. Fairmont Coal Co., 215 U.S. 349, 370–372, 30 S.Ct. 140, 54 L.Ed. 228; Black & White Taxicab, etc., Co. v. Brown & Yellow Taxicab, etc., Co., 276 U.S. 518, 532–536, 48 S.Ct. 404, 408, 409, 72 L.Ed. 681, 57 A.L.R. 426.

> 'But law in the sense in which courts speak of it today does not exist without some definite authority behind it. The common law so far as it is enforced in a State, whether called common law or not, is not the common law generally but the law of that State existing by the authority of that State without regard to what it may have been in England or anywhere else. * * *
>
> 'The authority and only authority is the State, and if that be so, the voice adopted by the State as its own (whether it be of its Legislature or of its Supreme Court) should utter the last word.'

Thus the doctrine of Swift v. Tyson is, as Mr. Justice Holmes said, 'an unconstitutional assumption of powers by the Courts of the United States which no lapse of time or respectable array of opinion should make us hesitate to correct.' In disapproving that doctrine we do not hold ***80** unconstitutional section 34 of the Federal Judiciary Act of 1789 or any other act of Congress. We merely declare that in applying the doctrine this Court and the lower courts have invaded rights which in our opinion are reserved by the Constitution to the several states.

Fourth. The defendant contended that by the common law of Pennsylvania as declared by its highest court in Falchetti v. Pennsylvania R. Co., 307 Pa. 203, 160 A. 859, the only duty owed to the plaintiff was to refrain from willful or wanton injury. The plaintiff denied that such is the Pennsylvania law.[24] In support of their respective contentions the parties discussed and cited many decisions of the Supreme Court of the state. The Circuit Court of Appeals ruled that the question of liability is one of general law; and on that ground declined to decide the issue of state law. As we hold this was error, the judgment is reversed and the case remanded to it for further proceedings in conformity with our opinion.

Reversed.

MR. JUSTICE CARDOZO took no part in the consideration or decision of this case.

MR. JUSTICE BUTLER (dissenting).

The case presented by the evidence is a simple one. Plaintiff was severely injured in Pennsylvania. While walking on defendant's right of way along a much-used path at the end of the cross-ties of its main track, he came into collision with an open door swinging from the side of a car in a train going in the opposite direction. Having been warned by whistle and headlight, he saw the locomotive ***81** approaching and had time and space enough to step aside and so avoid danger. To justify his failure to get out of

---

[24] Tompkins also contended that the alleged rule of the Falchetti Case is not in any event applicable here because he was struck at the intersection of the longitudinal pathway and a transverse crossing. The court below found it unnecessary to consider this contention, and we leave the question open.

the way, he says that upon many other occasions he had safely walked there while trains passed.

Invoking jurisdiction on the ground of diversity of citizenship, plaintiff, a citizen and resident of Pennsylvania, brought this suit to recover damages against defendant, a New York corporation, in the federal court for the Southern District of that state. The issues were whether negligence of defendant was a proximate cause of his injuries, and whether negligence of plaintiff contributed. He claimed that, by hauling the car with the open door, defendant violated a duty to him. The defendant insisted that it violated no duty, and that plaintiff's injuries were caused by his own ****824** negligence. The jury gave him a verdict on which the trial court entered judgment; the Circuit Court of Appeals affirmed. 2 Cir., 90 F.2d 603.

Defendant maintained, citing Falchetti v. Pennsylvania R. Co., 307 Pa. 203, 160 A. 859, and Koontz v. Baltimore & O.R. Co., 309 Pa. 122, 163 A. 212, that the only duty owed plaintiff was to refrain from willfully or wantonly injuring him; it argued that the courts of Pennsylvania had so ruled with respect to persons using a customary longitudinal path, as distinguished from one crossing the track. The plaintiff insisted that the Pennsylvania decisions did not establish the rule for which the defendant contended. Upon that issue the Circuit Court of Appeals said (90 F.2d 603, et page 604): 'We need not go into this matter since the defendant concedes that the great weight of authority in other states is to the contrary. This concession is fatal to its contention, for upon questions of general law the federal courts are free, in absence of a local statute, to exercise their independent judgment as to what the law is; and it is well settled that the question of the responsibility of a railroad for injuries caused by its servants is one of general law.' ***82** Upon that basis the court held the evidence sufficient to sustain a finding that plaintiff's injuries were caused by the negligence of defendant. It also held the question of contributory negligence one for the jury.

Defendant's petition for writ of certiorari presented two questions: Whether its duty toward plaintiff should have been determined in accordance with the law as found by the highest court of Pennsylvania, and whether the evidence conclusively showed plaintiff guilty of contributory negligence. Plaintiff contends that, as always heretofore held by this Court, the issues of negligence and contributory negligence are to be determined by general law against which local decisions may not be held conclusive; that defendant relies on a solitary Pennsylvania case of doubtful applicability, and that, even if the decisions of the courts of that state were deemed controlling, the same result would have to be reached.

No constitutional question was suggested or argued below or here. And as a general rule, this Court will not consider any question not raised below and presented by the petition. Olson v. United States, 292 U.S. 246, 262,

54 S.Ct. 704, 711, 78 L.Ed. 1236; Johnson v. Manhattan Ry. Co., 289 U.S. 479, 494, 53 S.Ct. 721, 726, 77 L.Ed. 1331; Gunning v. Cooley, 281 U.S. 90, 98, 50 S.Ct. 231, 234, 74 L.Ed. 720. Here it does not decide either of the questions presented, but, changing the rule of decision in force since the foundation of the government, remands the case to be adjudged according to a standard never before deemed permissible.

The opinion just announced states that: 'The question for decision is whether the oft-challenged doctrine of Swift v. Tyson (1842, 16 Pet. 1, 10 L.Ed. 865) shall now be disapproved.'

That case involved the construction of the Judiciary Act of 1789, s 34, 28 U.S.C.A. s 725: 'The laws of the several States, except where the Constitution, treaties, or statutes of the United States otherwise require or provide, shall be regarded as rules of decision in trials at common law, in the courts of ***83** the United States, in cases where they apply.' Expressing the view of all the members of the Court, Mr. Justice Story said (16 Pet. 1, at page 18, 10 L.Ed. 865): 'In the ordinary use of language, it will hardly be contended, that the decisions of courts constitute laws. They are, at most, only evidence of what the laws are, and are not, of themselves, laws. They are often reexamined, reversed, and qualified by courts themselves, whenever they are found to be either defective, or illfounded, or otherwise incorrect. The laws of a state are more usually understood to mean the rules and enactments promulgated by the legislative authority thereof, or long-established local customs having the force of laws. In all the various cases, which have hitherto come before us for decision, this court have uniformly supposed, that the true interpretation of the 34th section limited its application to state laws strictly local, that is to say, to the positive statutes of the state, and the construction thereof adopted by the local tribunals, and to rights and titles to things having a permanent locality, such as the rights and titles to real estate, and other matters immovable and intraterritorial in their nature and character. It never has been supposed by us, that the section did apply, or was designed to apply, to questions of a more general nature, not at all dependent upon local statutes or local usages of a fixed and permanent operation, as, for example, to the construction of ordinary contracts or ****825** other written instruments, and especially to questions of general commercial law, where the state tribunals are called upon to perform the like functions as ourselves, that is, to ascertain, upon general reasoning and legal analogies, what is the true exposition of the contract or instrument, or what is the just rule furnished by the principles of commercial law to govern the case. And we have not now the slightest difficulty in holding, that this section, upon its true intendment and construction, is strictly limited to local statutes and local usages of the character ***84** before stated, and does not extend to contracts and other instruments of a commercial nature, the true interpretation and effect whereof are to be sought, not in the decisions of the local tribunals, but in the general principles and doctrines of commercial jurisprudence. Undoubtedly, the decisions of the local tribunals upon such subjects are entitled to, and will receive, the most deliberate attention and respect of this court; but they cannot furnish positive rules or conclusive authority, by which our own judgments are to be bound up and governed.' (Italics added.)

The doctrine of that case has been followed by this Court in an unbroken line of decisions. So far as appears, it was not questioned until more than 50 years later, and then by a single judge.[1] Baltimore & O. Railroad Co. v. Baugh, 149 U.S. 368, 390, 13 S.Ct. 914, 37 L.Ed. 772. In that case, Mr. Justice Brewer, speaking for the Court, truly said (149 U.S. 368, at page 373, 13 S.Ct. 914, 916, 37 L.Ed. 772): 'Whatever differences of opinion may have been expressed have not been on the question whether a matter of general law should be settled by the independent judgment of this court, rather than through an adherence to the decisions of the state courts, but upon the other question, whether a given matter is one of local or of general law.'

And since that decision, the division of opinion in this Court has been of the same character as it was before. In 1910, Mr. Justice Holmes, speaking for himself and two other Justices, dissented from the holding that a ***85** court of the United States was bound to exercise its own independent judgment in the construction of a conveyance made before the state courts had rendered an authoritative decision as to its meaning and effect. Kuhn v. Fairmont Coal Co., 215 U.S. 349, 30 S.Ct. 140, 54 L.Ed. 228. But that dissent accepted (215 U.S. 349, at page 371, 30 S.Ct. 140, 54 L.Ed. 228) as 'settled' the doctrine of Swift v. Tyson, and insisted (215 U.S. 349, at page 372, 30 S.Ct. 140, 54 L.Ed. 228) merely that the case under consideration was by nature and necessity peculiarly local.

Thereafter, as before, the doctrine was constantly applied.[2] In Black & White Taxicab Co. v. Brown & Yellow Taxicab Co., 276 U.S. 518, 48 S.Ct. 404, 72 L.Ed. 681, 57 A.L.R. 426, three judges dissented. The writer of the dissent, Mr. Justice Holmes said, however (276 U.S. 518, at page 535, 48 S.Ct. 404, 409, 72 L.Ed. 681, 57 A.L.R. 426): 'I should leave Swift v. Tyson

---

1 Mr. Justice Field Filed a dissenting opinion, several sentences of which are quoted in the decision just announced. The dissent failed to impress any of his associates. It assumes that adherence to section 34 as construed involves a supervision over legislative or judicial action of the states. There is no foundation for that suggestion. Clearly, the dissent of the learned Justice rests upon misapprehension of the rule. He joined in applying the doctrine for more than a quarter of a century before his dissent. The reports do not disclose that he objected to it in any later case. Cf. Oakes v. Mase, 165 U.S. 363, 17 S.Ct. 345, 41 L.Ed. 746.

2 In Salem Co. v. Manufacturers' Co., 264 U.S. 182, at page 200, 44 S.Ct. 266, 271, 68 L.Ed. 628, 31 A.L.R. 867, Mr. Justice Holmes and Mr. Justice Brandeis concurred in the judgment of the Court upon a question of general law on the ground that the rights of the parties were governed by state law.

undisturbed, as I indicated in Kuhn v. Fairmont Coal Co., but I would not allow it to spread the assumed dominion into new fields.'

No more unqualified application of the doctrine can be found than in decisions of this Court speaking through Mr. Justice Holmes. United Zinc Co. v. Britt, 258 U.S. 268, 42 S.Ct. 299, 66 L.Ed. 615, 36 A.L.R. 28; Baltimore & O.R.R. Co. v. Goodman, 275 U.S. 66, 70, 48 S.Ct. 24, 25, 72 L.Ed. 167, 56 A.L.R. 645. Without in the slightest departing from that doctrine, but implicitly applying it, the strictness of the rule laid down in the Goodman Case was somewhat ameliorated by ****826** Pokora v. Wabash Ry. Co., 292 U.S. 98, 54 S.Ct. 580, 78 L.Ed. 1149, 91 A.L.R. 1049.

Whenever possible, consistently with standards sustained by reason and authority constituting the general law, this Court has followed applicable decisions of state courts. Mutual Life Co. v. Johnson, 293 U.S. 335, 339, 55 S.Ct. 154, 156, 79 L.Ed. 398. See Burgess v. Seligman, 107 U.S. 20, 34 2 S.Ct. 10, 27 L.Ed. 359; Black & White Taxicab Co. v. Brown & Yellow Taxicab Co., supra, 276 U.S. 518, at page 530, 48 S.Ct. 404, 407, 72 L.Ed. 681, 57 A.L.R. 426. Unquestionably, the determination of the issues of negligence and contributory negligence upon which decision of this case ***86** depends are questions of general law. Hough v. Texas Railway Co., 100 U.S. 213, 226, 25 L.Ed. 612; Lake Shore Railway Co. v. Prentice, 147 U.S. 101, 13 S.Ct. 261, 37 L.Ed. 97; Baltimore & O. Railroad Co. v. Baugh, supra; Gardner v. Michigan Central Railroad Co., 150 U.S. 349, 358, 14 S.Ct. 140, 37 L.Ed. 1107; Central Vermont Ry. Co. v. White, 238 U.S. 507, 512, 35 S.Ct. 865, 59 L.Ed. 1433, Ann.Cas.1916B, 252; Baltimore & O.R.R. Co. v. Goodman, supra; Pokora v. Wabash Ry. Co., supra.

While amendments to section 34 have from time to time been suggested, the section stands as originally enacted. Evidently Congress has intended throughout the years that the rule of decision as construed should continue to govern federal courts in trials at common law. The opinion just announced suggests that Mr. Warren's research has established that from the beginning this Court has erroneously construed section 34. But that author's 'New Light on the History of the Federal Judiciary Act of 1789' does not purport to be authoritative, and was intended to be no more than suggestive. The weight to be given to his discovery has never been discussed at this bar. Nor does the opinion indicate the ground disclosed by the research. In his dissenting opinion in the Taxicab Case, Mr. Justice Holmes referred to Mr. Warren's work, but failed to persuade the Court that 'laws' as used in section 34 included varying and possibly ill-considered rulings by the courts of a state on questions of common law. See, e.g., Swift v. Tyson, supra, 16 Pet. 1, 16, 17, 10 L.Ed. 865. It well may be that, if the Court should now call for argument of counsel on the basis of Mr. Warren's research, it would adhere to the construction it has always put upon section 34. Indeed, the opinion in this case so indicates. For it declares: 'If only a question of statutory construction were involved, we should not be prepared to abandon a doctrine so widely applied throughout nearly a century. But the unconstitutionality of the course pursued has now been made clear and compels us to do so.' This means that, so far as concerns the rule of decision now condemned, the Judiciary Act of 1789, passed to establish judicial ***87** courts to exert the judicial power of the United States, and especially section 34 of that act as construed, is unconstitutional; that federal courts are now bound to follow decisions of the courts of the state in which the controversies arise; and that Congress is powerless otherwise to ordain. It is hard to foresee the consequences of the radical change so made. Our opinion in the Taxicab Case cites numerous decisions of this Court which serve in part to indicate the field from which it is now intended forever to bar the federal courts. It extends to all matters of contracts and torts not positively governed by state enactments. Counsel searching for precedent and reasoning to disclose common-law principles on which to guide clients and conduct litigation are by this decision told that as to all of these questions the decisions of this Court and other federal courts are no longer anywhere authoritative.

This Court has often emphasized its reluctance to consider constitutional questions and that legislation will not be held invalid as repugnant to the fundamental law if the case may be decided upon any other ground. In view of grave consequences liable to result from erroneous exertion of its power to set aside legislation, the Court should move cautiously, seek assistance of counsel, act only after ample deliberation, show that the question is before the Court, that its decision cannot be avoided by construction of the statute assailed or otherwise, indicate precisely the principle or provision of the Constitutional held to have been transgressed, and fully disclose the reasons and authorities found to warrant the conclusion of invalidity. These safeguards against the improvident use of the great power to invalidate legislation are so well-grounded and familiar that statement of reasons or citation of authority to support them is no longer necessary. But see, e.g., ****827** Charles River Bridge v. Warren Bridge, 11 Pet. 420, 553, 9 L.Ed. 773; Township of Pine Grove v. Talcott, 19 Wall. 666, 673, 22 L.Ed. 227; Chicago, etc., Railway Co. v. Wellman, 143 U.S. 339, 345, 12 S.Ct. 400, 36 L.Ed. 176; ***88** Baker v. Grice, 169 U.S. 284, 292, 18 S.Ct. 323, 42 L.Ed. 748; Martin v. District of Columbia, 205 U.S. 135, 140, 27 S.Ct. 440, 51 L.Ed. 743.

So far as appears, no litigant has ever challenged the power of Congress to establish the rule as construed. It has so long endured that its destruction now without appropriate deliberation cannot be justified. There is nothing in the opinion to suggest that consideration of any constitutional question is necessary to a decision of the case. By way of reasoning, it contains nothing that requires the conclusion reached. Admittedly, there is no authority to support that conclusion. Against the protest of those joining in this opinion, the Court declines to assign the case for reargument. It may not justly be assumed that the labor and argument of counsel for the parties would not disclose the right conclusion and aid the Court in the statement of reasons to support it. Indeed, it would have been appropriate to give Congress opportunity to be heard before devesting it of power to prescribe rules of decision to be followed in the courts of the United States. See Myers v. United States, 272 U.S. 52, 176, 47 S.Ct. 21, 45, 71 L.Ed. 160.

The course pursued by the Court in this case is repugnant to the Act of Congress of August 24, 1937, 50 Stat. 751, 28 U.S.C.A. ss 17 and note, 349a, 380a and note, 401. It declares that: 'Whenever the constitutionality of any Act of Congress affecting the public interest is drawn in question in any court of the United States in any suit or proceeding to which the United States, or any agency thereof, or any officer or employee thereof, as such officer or employee, is not a party, the court having jurisdiction of the suit or proceeding shall certify such fact to the Attorney General. In any such case the court shall permit the United States to intervene and become a party for presentation of evidence (if evidence is otherwise receivable in such suit or proceeding) and argument upon the question of the constitutionality of such Act. In any such suit or proceeding the United States shall, subject to the applicable provisions of law, have all the rights of a ***89** party and the liabilities of a party as to court costs to the extent necessary for a proper presentation of the facts and law relating to the constitutionality of such Act.' Section 1, 28 U.S.C.A. s 401. That provision extends to this Court. Section 5, 28 U.S.C.A. s 380a note. If defendant had applied for and obtained the writ of certiorari upon the claim that, as now held, Congress has no power to prescribe the rule of decision, section 34 as construed, it would have been the duty of this Court to issue the prescribed certificate to the Attorney General in order that the United States might intervene and be heard on the constitutional question. Within the purpose of the statute and its true intent and meaning, the constitutionality of that measure has been 'drawn in question.' Congress intended to give the United States the right to be heard in every case involving constitutionality of an act affecting the public interest. In view of the rule that, in the absence of challenge of constitutionality, statutes will not here be invalidated on that ground, the Act of August 24, 1937 extends to cases where constitutionality is first 'drawn in question' by the Court. No extraordinary or unusual action by the Court after submission of the cause should be permitted to frustrate the wholesome purpose of that act. The duty it imposes ought here to be willingly assumed. If it were doubtful whether this case is within the scope of the act, the Court should give the United States opportunity to intervene and, if so advised, to present argument on the constitutional question, for undoubtedly it is one of great public importance. That would be to construe the act according to its meaning.

The Court's opinion in its first sentence defines the question to be whether the doctrine of Swift v. Tyson shall now be disapproved; it recites (third page, 58 S.Ct. 819) that Congress is without power to prescribe rules of decision that have been followed by federal courts as a result of the construction of section 34 in Swift v. Tyson and since; after discussion, it declares (seventh page, 58 S.Ct. 822) that 'the unconstitutionality of the course pursued (meaning the rule of decision ***90** resulting from that construction) * * * compels' abandonment of the doctrine so long applied; and then near the end of the last page, 58 S.Ct. 823, the Court states that it does not hold section 34 unconstitutional, but merely that, in applying the doctrine of Swift v. Tyson construing it, this Court and the lower courts have invaded rights which are reserved ****828** by the Constitution to the several states. But, plainly through the form of words employed, the substance of the decision appears; it strikes down as unconstitutional section 34 as construed by our decisions; it divests the Congress of power to prescribe rules to be followed by federal courts when deciding questions of general law. In that broad field it compels this and the lower federal courts to follow decisions of the courts of a particular state.

I am of opinion that the constitutional validity of the rule need not be considered, because under the law, as found by the courts of Pennsylvania and generally throughout the country, it is plain that the evidence required a finding that plaintiff was guilty of negligence that contributed to cause his injuries, and that the judgment below should be reversed upon that ground.

MR. JUSTICE MCREYNOLDS, concurs in this opinion.

MR. JUSTICE REED (concurring in part).

I concur in the conclusion reached in this case, in the disapproval of the doctrine of Swift v. Tyson, and in the reasoning of the majority opinion, except in so far as it relies upon the unconstitutionality of the 'course pursued' by the federal courts.

The 'doctrine of Swift v. Tyson,' as I understand it, is that the words 'the laws,' as used in section 34, line 1, of the Federal Judiciary Act of September 24, 1789, 28 U.S.C.A. s 725, do not included in their meaning 'the decisions of the local tribunals.' Mr. Justice Story, in deciding that point, said, 16 Pet. 1, 19, 10 L.Ed. 865: ***91** 'Undoubtedly, the decisions of the local tribunals upon such subjects are entitled to, and will receive, the most deliberate attention and respect of this court; but they cannot furnish positive rules, or conclusive authority, by which our own judgments are to be bound up and governed.'

To decide the case now before us and to 'disapprove' the doctrine of Swift v. Tyson requires only that we say that the words 'the laws' include in their meaning the decisions of the local tribunals. As the majority opinion shows, by its reference to Mr. Warren's researches and the first quotation from Mr. Justice Holmes, that this Court is now of the view that 'laws' includes 'decisions,' it is unnecessary to go further and declare that the 'course pursued' was 'unconstitutional,' instead of merely erroneous.

The 'unconstitutional' course referred to in the majority opinion is apparently the ruling in Swift v. Tyson that the supposed omission of Congress to legislate as to the effect of decisions leaves federal courts free to interpret general law for themselves. I am not at all sure whether, in the absence of federal statutory direction, federal courts would be compelled to follow state decisions. There was sufficient doubt about the matter in 1789 to induce the first Congress to legislate. No former opinions of this Court have passed upon it. Mr. Justice Holmes evidently saw nothing 'unconstitutional' which required the overruling of Swift v. Tyson, for he said in the very opinion quoted by the majority, 'I should leave Swift v. Tyson undisturbed, as I indicated in Kuhn v. Fairmont Coal Co., but I would not allow it to spread the assumed dominion into new fields.' Black & White Taxicab Co. v. Brown & Yellow Taxicab Co., 276 U.S. 518, 535, 48 S.Ct. 404, 409, 72 L.Ed. 681, 57 A.L.R. 426. If the opinion commits this Court to the position that the Congress is without power to declare what rules of substantive law shall govern the federal courts, ***92** that conclusion also seems questionable. The line between procedural and substantive law is hazy, but no one doubts federal power over procedure. Wayman v. Southard, 10 Wheat. 1, 6 L.Ed. 253. The Judiciary Article, 3, and the 'necessary and proper' clause of article 1, s 8, may fully authorize legislation, such as this section of the Judiciary Act.

In this Court, stare decisis, in statutory construction, is a useful rule, not an inexorable command. Burnet v. Coronado Oil & Gas Co., 285 U.S. 393, dissent, page 406, note 1, 52 S.Ct. 443, 446, 76 L.Ed. 815. Compare Read v. Bishop of Lincoln, (1892) A.C. 644, 655; London Street Tramways v. London County Council, (1898) A.C. 375, 379. It seems preferable to overturn an established construction of an act of Congress, rather than, in the circumstances of this case, to interpret the Constitution. Cf. United States v. Delaware & Hudson Co., 213 U.S. 366, 29 S.Ct. 527, 53 L.Ed. 836.

There is no occasion to discuss further the range or soundness of these few phrases of the opinion. It is sufficient now to call attention to them and express my own non-acquiescence.

CHAPTER 3

ANALYZING A STATUTORY LEGAL PROBLEM

■ ■ ■

1. INTRODUCTION

In this Chapter, you will see how a U.S. lawyer begins, executes, and finalizes a legal research project at her firm. You will be following along while Susan Cooke, an associate at a New York law firm, addresses a legal problem for one of her firm's clients. Maryanne Blackmun, a partner at the firm, will assign a research problem to Susan, and Susan will do legal research and evaluate the client's problem under the applicable law. You will then see the formal legal memorandum that Susan would write that analyzes the legal issues presented by the client's problem. By doing this, you will learn how you can write a formal legal memorandum about a new client's legal problem.

Lawyers (and law students) spend a lot of their time thinking about novel legal problems and predicting how a court would resolve them. In legal practice, lawyers first analyze facts, then they find relevant statutory and/or case law to apply to the facts. Finally, they present their analysis in an appropriate written form. Sometimes that written form is a formal legal memorandum, but often an associate simply drafts a well-organized email to the partner who assigned the problem to him.

In law school, students engage in this same process in their classes. Students read statutes and cases about some area of the law throughout the semester—for example torts or contracts or criminal law. Throughout the semester, the professor often asks students to use the cases discussed in class to analyze sample fact patterns to determine how a court is likely to resolve the legal issues that the fact patterns present. At the end of the semester, professors often give an exam that follows this same process. The professor creates one or two new fact patterns, and students use the cases that they have read during the semester to address the legal issues that the fact patterns present. The process for creating answers is similar to the process for creating the legal analyses that we will look at in this chapter.

Based on your experiences in this Chapter, you will be able to not only conduct your own legal research and to produce a formal legal memorandum on a new legal problem but you will also be able to write excellent law school exams. We will be using the law school exam as an example of how to address legal issues throughout this chapter. It is important for you to understand how U.S. law school prepares lawyers to practice law in the U.S. By engaging in the legal research and writing process, you can learn to be an excellent U.S. law student and an excellent U.S. lawyer.

2. CONSTRUCTING A LEGAL ANALYSIS

Whenever a lawyer (or a law student) begins thinking about a legal problem, he must first be sure that he understands the facts. Often, it will not be clear at first which facts are most relevant to the legal analysis. That is, until a lawyer understands what the law treats as a significant fact, a lawyer cannot decide which facts will be the most relevant to his legal analysis. In the beginning, a lawyer must assume that all facts are important. As he does legal research, it becomes clearer which facts are going to be legally significant.

In law school, professors take a similar approach to law school exams. The professor will give students very long fact patterns to analyze. Based on the student's understanding of all of the law that he has read and discussed in class throughout the semester, the students will be able to focus on the legally significant facts in the fact pattern. The reading and studying throughout the semester at law school is the equivalent to doing legal research at a law firm. In law school, the professor gives students the "research." In a law firm, the associate must go find it.

The goal is the same. By reading relevant case law, both lawyers and law students can evaluate which facts are legally significant for the legal analysis of the client's legal problem. The process of reading and understanding cases in law school classes prepares students to read relevant cases and to evaluate legally significant facts for clients in legal practice. In this chapter, you will observe while Susan does a little of both. First, Maryanne, the partner, will send an email to Susan, the associate, explaining the basic facts of the case. Then you can see how Susan begins her legal research and finally provides a legal analysis of the client's problem.

A. UNDERSTANDING THE FACTS OF THE CASE

In the beginning of any legal analysis, the lawyer (and the law student) will need to understand the factual situation that the client's case presents. Based on this initial understanding of the facts, he can begin to do legal research.

Read the email below sent by the partner to the senior associate. As you read the email, try to answer the following questions:

1. Who are the parties in this case?
2. What is the client complaining about?
3. Do you think that any important information is missing?
4. What is the legal issue that Susan will be researching?
5. Why do you think that the partner believes that NY law should apply here?

To: *Susan Cooke, Senior Associate*

From: *Maryanne Blackmun, Partner*

Re: *New York Box Company v. Manhattan Watch Company*

Susan:

Please take a look at this, and let me know what you think. I have given you a quick summary of the facts as I understand them, and I have also included the judge's decision in this case. The judge offered very little legal reasoning in his opinion, but he does cite some of the most relevant cases. After you read through the facts, please read the cases cited in the opinion. I have confirmed that the cases are the most relevant and that they are still good law. I want you to read them and then write a legal memorandum analyzing our client's case. Based on that, we can decide whether we should advise Jessica to appeal the judge's decision.

Here are the facts:

We now represent the New York Box Company (NYBC). NYBC is a New York corporation, with its headquarters and its only factory in New York City. NYBC makes boxes for shipping a variety of products. Manufacturers can order standard boxes, or they can have NYBC make customized boxes that conform to the buyer's specific requirements.

Manhattan Watch Company (MWC) is a manufacturer of traditional men's watches. MWC is a Delaware corporation, with its headquarters in New York and its principal factory in Switzerland. They make several different types of watches. They sell their watches in very distinctive boxes. Jordan Cooper is the MWC employee who is in charge of buying boxes for the watches made by MWC. Although he is satisfied with the present provider of boxes, he is always looking for something better.

One day while browsing the web for box manufacturers, Jordan found NYBC's website. He liked the NYBC boxes so much that he decided that he would like to switch box manufacturers and to work with NYBC. Jordan sent an email to Steven Ritts, who is the CEO of MWC, asking him to look at the NYBC website—he included a link to the site in his email.

While looking at the website, Steven Ritts noticed that the CEO of NYBC was Jessica Tandy. Steven had read about Jessica and how successful her company was.

Steven found Jessica's email address on her LinkedIn page and sent her an email inviting her to lunch.

Jessica replied, and the two CEOs met a few days later. At lunch, they agreed that their companies could do business together. They agreed that NYBC could deliver each month to MWC's warehouse in New York 10,000 boxes that would be designed to MWC's exact specifications. The price would be $10 per box. They also agreed that NYBC would send an invoice to MSC at the end of each month. Payment would be due by the 15th of the following month. It would be an initial three-year contract that the parties could extend by mutual agreement.

When Jessica got back to her office, she sent an email to Steven thanking him for lunch and setting out the details of their agreement. Steven responded to Jessica's email, agreeing with her characterization of their deal. Steven sent to Jessica the detailed specifications of the MWC boxes. She responded that NYBC would send a proto-type box for MWC's approval. In a couple of weeks, the proto-type box arrived at MWC, and everyone loved it. Steven emailed Jessica to tell her that she could begin shipping the boxes to MWC.

When NYBC sent the first order, it included an invoice that listed the number of boxes shipped, the total price of the shipment, and a statement that payment was due on the 15th of the following month. When the first shipment arrived at MWC, Steven personally inspected the boxes. When he was satisfied that the boxes conformed to their agreement, he authorized his accounting staff to send payment to NYBC.

When the accounting staff sent the payment to NYBC, it included a Confirmation form with the payment. The Confirmation stated that the order had arrived as agreed. On the front side of the Confirmation, MWC stated the number of boxes received and the condition of the boxes. On the back side of the Confirmation, MWC included three additional clauses: 1) a clause designating NY law as the applicable law of their contract; 2) an arbitration clause specifying that all disputes under the contract would be decided by arbitration in New York under the rules of the American Arbitration Association; and 3) a standard Force Majeure clause.

After a few days, Steven called Jessica to make sure that everything was OK on her end. He called her at her office and simply asked "Is everything OK?" Jessica had heard at a meeting that morning that the payment from MWC had arrived, and, based on that, Jessica responded "Yes, everything is fine. Thank you." It was a quick call.

The arrangement worked quite well for several months. MWC paid the first several invoices from NYBC. However, about nine months into their three-year contract, MWC complained to NYBC that it thought that the boxes were no longer as good as they were in the beginning. It demanded that NYBC go back to sending boxes that were like originals. NYBC assured MWC that the boxes were exactly the same and continued to ship 10,000 boxes per month and continued to send invoices for payment. MWC declined to pay the invoices; however, NYBC continued to send the boxes as agreed. NYBC's accounting department sent several messages to MWC, but they got no responses. Finally, Jessica hired a New York law firm to file suit in New York state court against MWC for breach of contract and failure to pay.

Soon after she filed the lawsuit, Jessica received a notice that MWC had filed a motion to the court to dismiss the case because the parties had agreed to arbitrate all disputes under their contract. The judge agreed with MWC that the Confirmations that MWC sent with its payments, which contained the arbitration clause, became part of the contract under New York UCC 2–207. The judge dismissed the case and ordered the parties to arbitrate.

Jessica would prefer to go before a judge in a court of law rather than to submit to an arbitration. Further, she says that she had no idea that the Confirmations that MWC had sent included the arbitration clause. The parties had never discussed arbitration, and she had never read the back side of the acknowledgments. She had never even read the front side. The accounting staff had simply filed the Confirmations in its MWC file.

Jessica wants to appeal the court's determination that the parties had agreed to arbitrate. I have attached the District Court order. Please research the relevant NY law and let me know whether Jessica has a good chance on appeal.

Thanks.

Maryanne

B. BEGINNING YOUR LEGAL RESEARCH

Maryanne has given Susan two great sources of information that will help her to start her legal research and her analysis of the client's problem: the facts of the case and the District Court's decision. Unless Susan is already familiar with the relevant law, it will probably be difficult for her to determine which of the facts in Maryanne's email will be legally significant in the analysis of the client's problem. Nonetheless, it is important that a lawyer knows as much as possible about the context of the legal problem. Researching the law will help Susan to focus on the important issues.

The first piece in the puzzle in this case is the District Court's opinion. The court has decided that the arbitration clause has become part of the parties' contract under the relevant NY law. Although Maryanne believes that the judge in this case has cited some authorities to support that conclusion, she does not think that the opinion provides sufficient legal analysis of the cases that the judge relies on. Susan must find the cases that the court cites and try to figure out how the court got to its decision. She will then have to find other relevant cases and other legal sources that will help her to evaluate her client's case. It could be that the District Court judge was correct in his analysis, or it could be that the District Court judge misinterpreted the law. Susan will have to start all over: she needs to think about the facts and research the law on her own.

Later in this Chapter, we will look at Susan's legal memorandum where she will provide a thorough legal analysis of the relevant law as applied to the facts of this case. A legal memorandum written by a lawyer and a legal opinion written by a judge are very different documents. The judge needs to decide the case and to provide some support for his decision. His primary role is to give a decision to the parties and to enter a judgment in the case. The lawyer, however, has a very different purpose in writing the legal memorandum. The associate's primary role is to explain the law to the partner so that the partner can advise the client.

The legal arguments in the judge's opinion are detailed enough to satisfy the parties and their lawyers that the judge has based his opinion on the law. However, the judge's analysis of the law is not detailed enough to satisfy the partner who is trying to provide legal advice to his client. Susan must thoroughly investigate all of the cases that relevant courts have decided in order to assure Maryanne that she can give the soundest legal advice to the client.

In all writing, it is essential that the writer satisfy the expectations of his reader. For the judge, his main readers are the parties and their lawyers; they want a judgment. For Susan, her main reader is Maryanne; Maryanne wants a thorough legal analysis of the client's case under the relevant law. As you read the judge's opinion, think about whether you think that his analysis is adequate for his audience (the parties) and whether his analysis is adequate for Susan's audience (Maryanne). Later in the Chapter, we will look at Susan's analysis in her legal memorandum and compare it to the judge's opinion. Although the audiences are different, each document is appropriate for its purpose.

C. IDENTIFYING RELEVANT SOURCES OF LAW

What follows is the opinion of U.S. District Court. As the partner explained, the District Court judge dismissed the NYBC suit because he concluded that the parties had agreed to arbitrate their disputes. He interpreted NY UCC 2–207(2) to mean that the arbitration clause that MWC included in its Confirmation became part of the parties' contract.

As you read the judge's opinion, notice that the judge does not fully explain his arguments. Instead, he simply makes legal conclusions and then provides citations to cases that he intends to support his conclusions. This type of writing is appropriate for the specific audiences for this document.

The primary audience for the judge's opinion includes the parties to the case and the parties' lawyers. The parties are mostly concerned with who won. Did the judge rule for the plaintiff or for the defendant? Most parties to lawsuits are not lawyers themselves, so they have little interest in the details of the judge's legal arguments. The parties' lawyers are interested in knowing what arguments the court found to be convincing, but, again, they are quite familiar with all of the possible arguments, so they only need the court to briefly explain which arguments were the most convincing and which cases the court relied on in the analysis.

This type of writing is very different from the type of writing that lawyers (and law students) do. When an associate (or a law student) is writing a legal memorandum, the primary audience is the partner who assigned the problem. The purpose in writing the memorandum is not to decide the case: that's what judges do. Neither the associate nor the partner is deciding the case. They are both lawyers who must advise clients about their legal options. When an associate is analyzing a legal problem in a legal memorandum for a partner in the firm, she must fully explain all of the possible arguments that could apply to the problem, and she must explain why one solution is more likely to be adopted by a court. The partner can then discuss this with the associate as a way to decide what legal advice to give to the client.

We will examine a legal memorandum later in this Chapter. First, however, let's look at the sources that Susan will use to create her legal analysis. The first document that she must read and understand is the opinion of the U.S. District Court. In this document, Susan can see how the court made its legal decision. However, the judge does not fully explain his decision. He is relying on the audience to "fill in" the details. Because the primary audience for this opinion is the parties and their lawyers, the judge can leave out some of the details of the analysis because the audience is so familiar with the relevant law and the facts of the case.

If the firm decides to represent this client, Maryanne would have to appeal this District Court ruling to the United States Circuit Court of Appeals for the 2nd Circuit in New York. The District Court opinion appears below. After Susan reads the opinion, she must evaluate the court's legal argument. To do this, she will have to read the sources that the judge cites in the opinion. First, let's look at the District Court opinion.

i. District Court Opinion

UNITED STATES DISTRICT COURT
SOUTHERN DISTRICT OF NEW YORK

NEW YORK BOX COMPANY, INC.,	:	
Plaintiff	:	10 Civ. 555 (DLC)
-v.-	:	
MANHATTAN WATCH COMPANY, INC.,	:	
Defendant.	:	

GEORGE TOWNE, DISTRICT JUDGE:

Facts

The Plaintiff, New York Box Company (NYBC), is a New York corporation with its headquarters in Manhattan. It manufactures its boxes in a factory in the Bronx. The Defendant, the Manhattan Watch Company (MWC) is a Delaware corporation with its headquarters in Manhattan. It manufacturers its watches in a factory in Geneva, Switzerland. MWC maintains a warehouse in New York. Because NYBC is a New York corporation, and MWC is a Delaware corporation, this court would have diversity jurisdiction in this case under 28 U.S.C.A. 1332.

The substance of the dispute would require this court to decide whether the Defendant breached its obligations to pay under the contract and whether the Plaintiff breached its obligations under the contract by providing sub-standard boxes that did not conform to the parties' contract.

Defendant, however, has filed a Motion to Dismiss, arguing that this Court does not have jurisdiction to decide the substance of this case because the parties have agreed to arbitrate all disputes under their contract pursuant to an arbitration clause contained in a Confirmation form sent by MWC to NYBC with its first payment.

The parties have agreed that all issues in this case are to be governed by New York law. Having reviewed the relevant cases applying New York law both by New York state courts and by federal courts applying New York law, I agree with the Defendant that the arbitration clause in the Confirmation is part of the parties' contract, and this court must dismiss this case in favor of arbitration.

Discussion

This is a classic "battle of the forms" case arising under NY UCC 2–207:

§ 2–207. Additional Terms in Acceptance or Confirmation

(1) A definite and seasonable expression of acceptance or a written confirmation which is sent within a reasonable time operates as an acceptance even though it states terms additional to or different from those offered or agreed upon, unless acceptance is expressly made conditional on assent to the additional or different terms.

(2) The additional terms are to be construed as proposals for addition to the contract. Between merchants such terms become part of the contract unless:

a. the offer expressly limits acceptance to the terms of the offer;

b. they materially alter it; or

c. notification of objection to them has already been given or is given within a reasonable time after notice of them is received.

(3) Conduct by both parties which recognizes the existence of a contract is sufficient to establish a contract for sale although the writings of the parties do not otherwise establish a contract. In such case the terms of the particular contract consist of those terms on which the writings of the parties agree, together with any supplementary terms incorporated under any other provisions of this Act.

Courts understand that UCC 2–207 was enacted to acknowledge that parties often make contracts using a number of related writings. The UCC sometimes steps in to fill in gaps that the parties leave in their negotiations. The UCC relies heavily on business practices among merchants to determine when contract provisions can be assumed to be part of the parties' contract.

The New York Court of Appeals had ruled in *Marlene* that an arbitration clause would always be a material alteration to a contract. *Marlene Industries, Corp. v. Carnac Textiles, Inc.* 380 NE 2nd 239 (New York 1978). The court distinguished arbitration clauses from all other types of clauses that parties might try to incorporate into their contracts through a "battle of the forms." The U.S. Supreme Court, however, interpreted the Federal Arbitration Act to prohibit state law from treating arbitration clauses any differently from other contract clauses. *Perry v. Thomas,* 482 U.S. 483 (1987).

After *Perry*, the New York courts must decide in each case whether the arbitration clause in the specific case would be a material alteration to the parties contract under UCC 2–207(2).

Applying New York law, the Second Circuit Court of Appeals has decided several cases quite similar to the case before this court. In *Aceros Prefabricados v. Tradearbed,* 282 F. 3rd 92 (2nd Cir. 2002), the court found that arbitration clauses were standard practice in the steel industry, and, therefore, the arbitration clause would not be a surprise. Based on that finding, and because there was no evidence to dispute this claim, the court found that the arbitration clause would not materially alter this contract. *Aceros* at 95.

Similarly, in *Chelsea Square Textiles v. Bombay Dyeing Company,* 189 F. 3rd 289 (2nd Cir. 1999), the court was considered an arbitration clause that was written in ungrammatical English and was printed on thin paper that made it difficult to read. The court first ruled that there was no evidence offered by the party objecting to the arbitration clause that arbitration clauses would be surprising in the textile industry. Further, the court ruled that the parties could figure out what the clauses said and that, because they were common in the textile industry, the arbitration clause would not be a material alteration to the contract. *Chelsea* at 193.

Like in *Aceros* and *Chelsea Textiles*, the parties to the contract in this case are experienced merchants, and no one has submitted any evidence that arbitration clauses are not common in their industry.

Under UCC 2–207 (2), we find that the arbitration clause is included in the parties' contract. Because the parties have agreed to arbitrate their disputes under this arbitration clause, this court has no jurisdiction to hear this case.

The case is Dismissed.

ii. Using the Legal Opinion to Focus Legal Research

Although the judge gave very little explanation for his decision, Susan can learn a great deal by reading the District Court's legal opinion. Because Susan had been an excellent law student, the facts of this case sounded familiar to her. She recalled from her first-year contracts class that her professor had mentioned something about cases like this. In fact, she seems to think that the professor asked a question about this on her final exam. The issue here seems to be whether the clauses in the Confirmation become part of the contract between NYBC and MWC. If those clauses do become part of the contract, then the District Court judge was correct to dismiss the case and to order arbitration. If the clauses in the Confirmation do not become part of the contract, then the District Court judge was incorrect, and NYBC could win on appeal.

Notice that Susan is not interested in whether MWC was in any sense justified in withholding payment from NYBC or whether either party breached the terms of their contract: either NYBC by sending non-conforming boxes, or MWC by failing to pay the monthly invoices. The issue here is whether the parties have agreed to arbitrate these disputes.

Susan vaguely recalled that this type of problem was called a "battle of the forms" problem. That is, the parties disagree about whether the Confirmations sent by MWC become part of the parties' contract under the relevant law.

The District Court opinion tells Susan many very valuable things: 1) it gives her the text of the relevant statutory law: UCC 2–207; 2) it tells her which cases that the court primarily relied upon to make its decision:

Chelsea Textiles and *Aceros Prefabricados*; and 3) it cites some other cases and legal sources that the court also relied upon to make its decision. The court, however, did not really analyze the cases in the opinion in enough detail to provide a thorough legal analysis of the client's case.

Although the judge might get an "A" for this document as a court opinion, he would probably get a "C" for this document as a legal memorandum or a law school exam. This is a good start for Susan's research, but she has a lot of work to do.

3. ANALYZING RELEVANT CASE LAW

From the judge's opinion, it is clear that the judge relied heavily on two opinions to support his decision: *Aceros* and *Chelsea*. Unfortunately, Susan has a very different audience and purpose from the judge. Susan must do more than simply provide a winner and a loser; she must do more than simply drop citations to cases that support one argument over another. Susan must provide a full legal analysis. Maryanne will eventually have to give legal advice to NYBC about whether it should appeal the judge's ruling. Susan needs to provide a legal analysis that will give Maryanne confidence that she has looked at all of the relevant law and that she has analyzed the client's legal situation in light of the precedent.

Before believing the judge that the *Aceros* and *Chelsea* cases are the most important precedent on the subject, Susan will have to do her own research. Although the appellate court judge will be somewhat interested in the lower court's legal argument, it will be deciding the case on its own: *de novo*. Susan will read all of the cases that are cited in the District Court opinion, and she will also read all of the cases that are cited in the *Aceros* and *Chelsea* cases. She would also do her own independent legal research.

After doing all of that legal research, Susan would probably conclude that the District Court was correct to rely on the *Aceros* and *Chelsea* cases. Susan would then read these two cases very carefully to try to determine for herself how these cases could be applied to the *NYBC v. MWC* case. Both cases are reproduced below. Susan must read these cases carefully to try to determine what the courts in those cases found to be legally significant to the analysis.

A. USING THE COMMON LAW ARGUMENT GUIDE

Let's start with the *Aceros* case and then the *Chelsea* case. As you read these cases, try to read them as Susan would read them. That is, try to think about the NYBC case. Try to answer the following questions, referring to the Common Law Argument Guide—reproduced below. Also, as you read the cases, also consult the comments on the right hand side of the page:

Common Law Argument Guide

Whenever you are reading U.S. common law legal arguments in any form of U.S. Legal English-cases; law review articles; legal memorandums, you must evaluate the writer's common law arguments. The writer should make it easy for you to see how his legal conclusions are supported by the legal sources that he discusses and cites. That is, you must evaluate whether the writer has given you enough information in order to determine whether his common law arguments are successful and convincing. As you read U.S. common law arguments, try to focus on the following things:

1) **Precedent.** Think about how the writer has chosen the statutes and cases that are being used to support his legal conclusions. Are they from the appropriate jurisdiction? Are they state law or are they federal law? Are the cases from the highest court in the jurisdiction or from a lower court?

2) **Analogy.** Think about how the writer has used the legally significant facts in the cases that are cited. Has he explained how the legally significant facts in these cases are either similar to or different from the facts of the case that the writer is discussing?

3) **Legal Issue(s).** Think about the primary legal issues that the writer is addressing. Are these legal issues the same as those in the cases that the writer is citing? How are they the same or different?

4) **Legal Reasoning.** Think about the rationale the courts used in deciding the cited cases that the writer is discussing; that is, has the writer explained how each court applied the law to the facts in each case?

5) **Legal Conclusions.** Think about the writer's legal conclusions on the points that he is addressing. Has the writer convinced you that his legal conclusions are supported by the applicable law?

i. *Aceros Prefabricados v. Tradearbed*[1]

MINER, CIRCUIT JUDGE

* * *

BACKGROUND

On December 17, 1999, TA, an affiliate of the world's largest steel manufacturer, and Aceros, a major Central American contractor, began exchanging letters, most of them written in Spanish, in connection with Aceros' prospective purchase of steel from TA. This correspondence included a list from Aceros of the products it desired, and several purchase orders from Aceros that included tonnages and proposed prices. The parties agree that, prior to the January 12 letter from TA to Aceros, no contract had been formed. They disagree, however, as to the significance of the January 12 letter. The January 12 letter states that TA "hereby confirm[s] the orders for beams as follows." The parties dispute the proper English translation of the letter's next sentence. Aceros asserts that it reads: "We hereby confirm that the above-mentioned orders will be shipped in the next few days." In contrast, TA contends that the correct translation is: "The confirmations of the above-mentioned orders will be shipped in the next few days."

> How do the facts of this case compare to the facts of the *NYBC v. MWC* case? Are the differences significant to the legal analysis? That is, do you think that this case is analogous to the *NYBC v. MWC* case on its facts?

Aceros argues that the January 12 letter demonstrates TA's intent to contract and therefore constituted an acceptance of Aceros' prior offers, resulting in a binding contract between the parties as of that date. TA maintains that it accepted Aceros' offers only when it sent three confirmation orders dated January 17, 2000, January 28, 2000, and March 9, 2000, that each confirmation constituted a separate acceptance, and that the parties therefore entered into three distinct contracts for the sale and purchase of steel. Each of the three confirmation orders was sent with a cover sheet stating that the confirmation "includes the sale terms and conditions for the [steel]", and the last page of each confirmation order contains a "[n]ote" that provides: "Subject to terms stated on General

[1] 282 F. 3rd 92 (2nd Cir. 2002).

Conditions of Sale enclosed. Your failure to object to any term within 10 days of receipt of this contract shall be deemed an acceptance by you." Aceros contends, and TA does not dispute, that the General Conditions of Sale were not included with any of the three confirmation orders. Nonetheless, the General Conditions of Sale contain the following arbitration provision: "Any controversy arising under or in connection with the contract shall be submitted to arbitration in New York City in accordance with the rules then obtaining of the American Arbitration Association." Aceros did not sign or return the January 17 confirmation, and it is undisputed that Aceros never objected to any term in any of the confirmation orders. It is also undisputed that an Aceros agent accepted the January 28 confirmation order, by writing "[a]ceptado" on and signing each of the four pages of the confirmation order and then mailing it back to TA. As with the first confirmation order, Aceros neither signed nor returned the third confirmation order dated March 9.

On December 11, 2000, Aceros commenced this diversity action against TA for breach of contract. On January 5, 2001, relying on the arbitration clause, TA moved to stay the action pending arbitration pursuant to section 3 of the FAA or to dismiss the action pursuant to Rule 12 of the Federal Rules of Civil Procedure. Aceros responded that the arbitration clause was not part of the parties' agreement as memorialized on January 12 because the General Conditions of Sale were (1) not accepted by Aceros; (2) not incorporated by reference into the confirmation orders; and (3) not enclosed with the confirmation orders as the orders themselves stated.

In a memorandum and order dated March 27, 2001, the district court denied TA's motion. *Aceros,* 2001 WL 303731, at *3. The court found that the January 12 letter evidenced the formation of a contract between the parties because while all prior correspondence from TA to Aceros contained language indicating an intent not to be bound, such as "pending confirmation from our principals" or "pending confirmation from our main office," the January 12 letter did not contain any similarly limiting ***97** language. *Id.* at *2. In reaching its conclusion, the court relied, without explanation, on Aceros' translation of the disputed confirmation language. Having found a contract formed by the January 12 letter, the court viewed the terms of the January 17, January 28, and March 9

> How does this District Court analysis differ from the one in the *NYBC v. MWC* case?

confirmation orders—among them, the requirement to arbitrate disputes—as proposals for additional terms to the contract. *Id.* Without any mention of Aceros' acceptance of the January 28 confirmation order, the court held, as a matter of law, that an arbitration provision materially alters legal rights under a contract, and therefore that the arbitration clause was not part of the parties' agreement. *Id.*

On April 4, 2001, TA filed a motion requesting that the court reconsider its order denying TA's motion to stay the case pending arbitration. In seeking reconsideration, TA contended that the district court erroneously relied on Aceros' translation of the January 12 letter rather than the translation offered in an affidavit of TA's vice president. In a memorandum and order dated April 23, 2001, the district court denied the motion for reconsideration. The court held that (1) the "self-serving affidavit of [TA's vice president] does not undermine the Court's reliance on the translation provided by [Aceros]," and (2) even under TA's proposed translation, "the language not disputed is sufficient to support" the court's denial of TA's motion to stay the proceedings. *Aceros Prefabricados,* 2001 WL 428245, at *1. This interlocutory appeal followed.

* * *

DISCUSSION

We have jurisdiction to hear this interlocutory appeal pursuant to section 16(a) of the FAA.[3] We review *de novo* the district court's legal conclusion that the parties did not contractually bind themselves to arbitrate disputes, *Chelsea Square Textiles, Inc. v. Bombay Dyeing & Manufacturing Co.,* 189 F.3d 289, 295 (2d Cir.1999), and review factual findings underlying those conclusions for clear error. *Id.* In regard to the contract at issue, we apply New York law.[4]

We therefore turn to an examination of whether the arbitration provisions are part of the parties' contract pursuant to section

---

[3] Section 16(a) provides that "[a]n appeal may be taken from . . . an order . . . refusing a stay of any action under section 3 of this title." 9 U.S.C. § 16(a)(1)(A).

[4] The parties' briefs assume that New York substantive law governs the issues of contract formation presented here, and such "implied consent . . . is sufficient to establish choice of law." *Krumme v. WestPoint Stevens Inc.,* 238 F.3d 133, 138 (2d Cir.2000) (quotation marks and citation omitted).

2–207(2).[7] It is undisputed that both TA and Aceros are merchants for the purposes of the UCC. *See id.* § 2–104(1). Under the UCC, proposed additional terms become part of a contract between merchants unless one of three statutory exceptions is satisfied. *See id.* § 2–207(2).[8] Aceros invokes only the "material alteration" exception of section 2–207(2)(b), which prohibits inclusion in a contract of a proposed additional term that would "materially alter" the contract unless the other party agrees. *Id.* § 2–207(2)(b). Aceros agreed to arbitrate disputes in regard to goods shipped under the January 28 confirmation order when it wrote "[a]ceptado" on and signed every page of that confirmation order and mailed it back to TA.[9] Aceros therefore bound itself to arbitrate disputes arising out of that order of goods. In contrast, neither the January 17 nor the March 9 confirmation order was expressly accepted by Aceros, and we must therefore determine whether the arbitration clause, as a proposed additional term in those two confirmation orders, is included in the parties' contract.

> The fact that Aceros accepted the January 28 confirmation makes this case different from the *NYBC v. MWC* case. Pay attention to the court's argument in this case. Does this fact ultimately matter to the court's decision?

[7] For the sake of clarity, we refer to the contractual status between the parties as involving a single "contract" with the understanding that this designation also encompasses the theory that the confirmation orders formed three separate contracts.

[8] Section 2–207(2) of the UCC provides:

(2) The additional terms are to be construed as proposals for addition to the contract. Between merchants such terms become part of the contract unless:

(a) the offer expressly limits acceptance to the terms of the offer;

(b) they materially alter it; or

(c) notification of objection to them has already been given or is given within a reasonable time after notice of them is received.

N.Y. U.C.C. § 2–207(2).

[9] Aceros claims that even this acceptance is ineffective to bind it to arbitrate disputes as to that shipment of goods because it did not sign "in the space provided as required by [TA's] order confirmation form." We reject this argument. The last page of the order contains the "[n]ote" that subjects the order to the General Conditions of Sale. At the end of the note are the words "ACCEPTED BY:". Rather than signing the order in the small space provided, an Aceros agent wrote "[a]ceptado" and signed his name less than two inches above that particular location. This is clearly an effective acceptance of that confirmation order and all the terms incorporated by reference. In any event, even if Aceros had not expressly accepted this confirmation order, it would nonetheless be bound to arbitration for the same reasons it is bound as to the other two confirmation orders.

"[T]he burden of proving the materiality of the alteration must fall on the party that opposes inclusion." *Bayway Ref.*, 215 F.3d at 223. This is so because the UCC presumes that between merchants additional terms will be included in a contract. *Id.* Thus, "if neither party introduced any evidence, the [proposed additional term] would, by the plain language of § 2–207(2), become part of the contract." *Id.* Aceros was therefore required to establish that the arbitration provision constituted a material alteration to its contract with TA.

A material alteration is one that would "result in surprise or hardship if incorporated without express awareness by the other party." N.Y. U.C.C. § 2–207 cmt. 4; *Bayway Ref.*, 215 F.3d at 224. Surprise includes both a subjective element of what a party actually knew and an objective element of what a party should have known. *Id.* We have stated that "[a] profession of surprise and raised eyebrows are not enough." *Id.* Instead, "[t]o carry [its] burden . . . [the nonassenting] party must establish that, under the circumstances, it cannot be presumed that a reasonable merchant would have consented to the additional term." *Id.*

> The court seems to rely on this *Bayway* case for some important legal conclusions. Susan should read this case.

Aceros has failed to submit any evidence demonstrating either subjective or objective surprise at the inclusion of an arbitration clause in its contract with TA. Aceros' sole reference to either surprise or hardship is supplied in an affidavit of its founder and general manager stating that "the addition of an arbitration clause ***101** which [Aceros] did not accept and never saw until long after the parties had negotiated the terms and entered into their contract would result in surprise and hardship to [Aceros]." This conclusory, unsupported statement falls far short of meeting the burden of proof required to show surprise and therefore the materiality of a proposed additional term. *Id.* at 224–25. In the absence of any evidence indicating Aceros' surprise as to the inclusion of the arbitration provision, it has

> Again, the court is relying on the *Bayway* case.

failed to establish that such a provision constitutes a material alteration of the contract. In a footnote in its brief on appeal, Aceros "submits that surprise and hardship are self-evident where, as here, there was no reference to nor mention by [TA] to arbitration until after suit was filed." This claim ignores the fact that Aceros has the burden of *establishing* the elements of surprise or hardship, not merely stating that they are present. As with the statement in the affidavit, this assertion is conclusory and unsupported by any evidence in the record.

In *Bayway Refining,* we noted that while Official Comment 4 to section 2–207 seems to suggest that hardship is an independent ground for finding that an alteration is material, there are cases indicating that hardship is not an element separate from surprise but rather a "consequence" of material alteration. *Id.* at 226 (citing *Union Carbide Corp. v. Oscar Mayer Foods Corp.*, 947 F.2d 1333, 1336 (7th Cir.1991); *Suzy Phillips Originals, Inc. v. Coville, Inc.*, 939 F.Supp. 1012, 1017 (E.D.N.Y.1996); and *In re Chateaugay Corp.*, 162 B.R. 949, 957 (Bankr.S.D.N.Y.1994)). We declined in *Bayway Refining* to decide whether hardship is an independent ground in the material alteration analysis because even if it were, the party resisting arbitration there failed to raise a genuine issue of material fact as to hardship sufficient to survive a motion for summary judgment. Likewise, here we need not make such a determination because—for the same reason Aceros has failed to establish surprise, the lack of any evidence supporting this claim—it has also failed to establish that it would suffer any hardship in being bound to arbitration.

> Again, the court here is simply leaving clues about what authorities support its legal conclusions in this case. Susan must read these cases and explain these authorities to Maryanne.

Moreover, TA's vice-president submitted an affidavit indicating that he has been employed in the steel business for more than thirty years and that "[a]rbitration clauses, like the one here, are commonplace and the norm in the industry and have been for a very long time." Aceros did not rebut this assertion. Under New York law, an arbitration agreement does not result in surprise or hardship where arbitration is the custom and practice within the relevant industry. *See Chelsea Square Textiles,* 189 F.3d at 296 ("[E]vidence of trade usage and course of dealings between parties supported . . . finding of an agreement to arbitrate.") (citing *Leadertex, Inc. v. Morganton Dyeing & Finishing Corp.,* 67 F.3d 20, 25 (2d Cir.1995)); *Schubtex,* 49 N.Y.2d at 6, 399 N.E.2d 1154, 424 N.Y.S.2d 133 ("[A] provision for arbitration [can] . . . be implied from a course of past conduct or the custom and practice in the industry."). The logic of this rule is obvious: a merchant in a given industry will have, by definition, a difficult time establishing either subjective or objective "surprise" regarding a proposed contract term that is standard in that industry.

> What does this discussion tell Susan about the *NYBC v. MWC* case? How will Susan determine whether arbitration is common in this industry?

The Official Comments to section 2–207 recognize the importance of trade practices to the material alteration analysis. Official Comment 4 lists "typical clauses which would normally 'materially alter' the contract and so result in surprise or hardship." N.Y. U.C.C. § 2–207 cmt. 4. A provision to arbitrate disputes is not among them. While the list is not exhaustive, the ***102** common thread among the examples provided is that they all constitute provisions that significantly deviate from industry norms. *See id.; see also Daisy Indust. v. Kmart Corp.,* No. 96 CIV. 4211, 1999 WL 1043964, at *8 (S.D.N.Y. Nov. 17, 1999) ("Most of the examples set forth in the comment significantly alter standard industry practice such that a party not used to operating under the additional terms would be surprised."); *Suzy Phillips Originals, Inc. v. Coville, Inc.,* 939 F.Supp. 1012, 1017 (E.D.N.Y.1996) ("[The] examples of clauses which materially alter a contract . . . all . . . have in common that they significantly alter standard industry practice and thus could surprise a buyer who would not have expected to be operating under such terms."). Conversely, among the "[e]xamples of clauses which involve no element of unreasonable surprise,"

Official Comment 5 lists proposed terms that are "within customary limits," "within the range of trade practice[s]," and "within . . . customary trade tolerances." N.Y. U.C.C. § 2–207 cmt. 5.

Although most of our cases that discuss trade usage in the context of section 2–207(2)(b) disputes deal with the textile industry, *see, e.g.*, *Chelsea Square Textiles*, 189 F.3d 289; *Pervel Indust., Inc. v. T M Wallcovering, Inc.*, 871 F.2d 7 (2d Cir.1989), there is nothing in those cases or in the UCC to indicate that consideration of trade usage is limited to that industry. *Cf. Bayway Ref.*, 215 F.3d at 225 (finding that proposed additional term was part of the parties' contract because inclusion of such term was commonplace in the petroleum industry). Indeed, the importance of industry practices in the interpretation of contracts for the sale of goods permeates the entire UCC. *See* James J. White & Robert S. Summers, *Uniform Commercial Code* § 3–3 (2d ed. 1980). This is clear from its definition of "usage of trade": "A usage of trade is any practice or method of dealing having such regularity of observance in a place, vocation or trade as to justify an expectation that it will be observed with respect to the transaction in question." N.Y. U.C.C. § 1–205(2). Moreover, "it is not necessary for both parties to be consciously aware of the trade usage. It is enough if the trade usage is such as to 'justify an expectation' of its observance." White & Summers, *supra*. Furthermore, "[usage of trade is] relevant not only to the interpretation of express contract terms, but may [itself] constitute contract terms." *Id.* Thus, standard industry practices are always relevant when interpreting contracts governed by the UCC, and Aceros failed to rebut TA's assertion that arbitration provisions are commonplace in the steel industry.

Susan should look at this source as well. It might contain a discussion of several relevant cases.

Aceros did not submit any evidence of surprise or hardship and therefore has failed to demonstrate that the inclusion of an arbitration provision in its contract with TA constitutes a material alteration under section 2–207(2)(b). Moreover, TA submitted unrebutted evidence that arbitration is standard practice within the steel industry, thereby precluding Aceros from establishing surprise or hardship. Accordingly, we hold that the arbitration provisions proposed in TA's confirmation orders became part of the contract, and that Aceros and TA are therefore required to arbitrate their disputes.

What does this case tell you about how a court might decide the NYBC case? In her memorandum, Susan must explain to Maryanne not only how to apply the reasoning of this case to the facts in the NYBC case but she must also explain to Maryanne what the courts are doing generally when they are interpreting UCC 2–207(2). To do that, she must read more cases.

CONCLUSION

For the foregoing reasons, the order appealed from is vacated, and the action is remanded to the district court for further proceedings consistent with this opinion.

ii. *Chelsea Square v. Bombay Dyeing*[2]

JOHN M. WALKER, JR. CIRCUIT JUDGE:

Defendant-appellant Bombay Dyeing and Manufacturing Company, Ltd. brings this interlocutory appeal pursuant to § 16(a) of the Federal Arbitration Act ("FAA"), 9 U.S.C. § 1 *et seq.*, from a July 23, 1998 order of the district court (Charles L. Brieant, *District Judge*). In its order, the district court denied Bombay Dyeing's motion to dismiss or stay the action and to compel arbitration in India and granted the cross-motion of plaintiffs-appellees Chelsea Square Textiles, Inc. ("Chelsea"), Kenneth Lazar, and Lester Gribetz (collectively, "the Chelsea Square plaintiffs") to enjoin the arbitration initiated by Bombay Dyeing in India. For the reasons that follow, we vacate the district court's stay of arbitration, reverse its decision denying Bombay Dyeing's motion to stay this action and compel arbitration, and direct the parties to proceed to arbitration pursuant to the rules of the Cotton Textile Export Promotion Council ("Texprocil") in Bombay, India.

I. BACKGROUND

This case concerns the enforceability of an arbitration clause that appears on standardized sales confirmation forms used by an Indian textile manufacturer, Bombay Dyeing, in its trade with an American textile

---

2 189 F. 3rd 289 (2nd Cir. 1999).

importer, producer, and re-seller, Chelsea Square Textiles, Inc. This appeal would present few difficulties if not for the fact that the arbitration clause at issue is so faint as to be nearly illegible and is so ***291** garbled as to be almost unintelligible. Some much-needed background follows.

A. *Prior Business Dealings*

Defendant-appellant Bombay Dyeing is an Indian corporation that manufactures and sells textiles throughout the world. Pursuant to Indian government regulations, all Indian textile companies, before they can export textiles, must obtain a Registration Cum Membership Certificate ("RCMC") from Texprocil, an agency sponsored by the Indian government. To obtain an RCMC, a company must agree to abide by a code of conduct and to use standard contract terms prescribed by Texprocil with respect to sales to overseas buyers. Among the standard terms and conditions required to be used by the exporting companies are those providing for the arbitration of all disputes arising from such contracts in accordance with the rules of arbitration set forth by Texprocil. It is not surprising, then, that arbitration has become a standard and customary trade practice for resolving disputes arising out of Indian textile exports.

Bombay Dyeing has used a standard "Confirmation of Cloth Sales" form (the "Confirmation") for all of its textile sales to overseas buyers for over twenty years. Typically, contracts for sale are consummated when Bombay Dyeing receives a purchase order from an overseas buyer and issues a Confirmation in response. The Confirmation bears the following legend: "We hereby confirm having sold to you goods as detailed below on the terms and conditions as stated herein and as printed overleaf." As suggested by the legend, printed on the back of the Confirmation are twenty-two paragraphs detailing the terms and conditions of the sale. These terms and conditions have remained largely unchanged over time, though the precise wording (and, in some instances, spelling or grammar) has varied. In English, paragraph 13 of the standard Confirmation's terms and conditions provides (all errors in original):

> All dispute and questions whatsoever which shall arise between the parties hereto out of or in connection with this contract of as to the construction of application thereof or the respective rights and obligation of the parties hereunder clause of thing herein contain or any account of valuation be made hereunder or as to any other matter in any way relating to these presents shall be referred to arbitration in accordance with rules for the time being in force as applicable to piece goods for export and which will be framed by The Cotton Textile Export Promotion Council in consultation with the Mills & Exporter Representatives selected in accordance with the provision therein. Nothing in the rules or

> arbitration or any implication thereof which runs counter to the terms and conditions of the contract shall be applied thereto.[1]

Beginning sometime in the late 1980s or early 1990s, Bombay Dyeing began doing business with James Pitts, who headed the North American division of a Japanese company called Kosen, Inc. While Pitts was employed at Kosen, Bombay Dyeing negotiated more than a thousand contracts with the company. In an evidentiary hearing held by the district court, Pitts testified that, on occasion, he saw Confirmation forms Bombay Dyeing sent in response to purchase orders submitted by Kosen.

In late 1991, Pitts left Kosen to found and become Chief Executive Officer of Rose Hill Linen Corporation. Pitts's wife, Nancy Pitts, was the Chief Operating Officer of Rose Hill. James Pitts testified that in its five years of existence, Rose Hill negotiated hundreds of contracts with Bombay Dyeing and a company he thought was Bombay Dyeing's corporate parent, Nowrosjee Wadia & Sons Ltd. ("Wadia"),[2] ***292** and that he personally saw Bombay Dyeing's Confirmations during that time. Pitts also acknowledged that he had signed at least one Confirmation from Wadia.[3]

Rose Hill subsequently filed for bankruptcy sometime in 1995. In early 1996, Pitts approached Bombay Dyeing's overseas sales agent to ascertain Bombay Dyeing's capacity for selling large quantities of textiles (250,000 to 500,000 yards) within a short time-frame to a new purchaser. Shortly thereafter, Pitts, along with plaintiffs Kenneth Lazar and Lester Gribetz, formed Chelsea Square Textiles, Inc., with substantial capital contributions from Lazar and Gribetz.[4] Although there is some dispute in the record, it appears that Nancy Pitts also worked for Chelsea as an "officer manager" of sorts.

---

1 As we state below, the version of paragraph 13 that appears in the Confirmation forms at issue in Bombay Dyeing's dispute with Chelsea varies slightly from the standard text.

2 The record is silent on the actual relationship between Bombay Dyeing and Wadia. However, the Confirmation forms sent by Wadia are almost identical to those identified above as Bombay Dyeing's standard Confirmation form. Moreover, the Confirmation forms list what appears to be an identical address for both Wadia and Bombay Dyeing.

3 The Wadia Confirmation form has the same legend on the front of the form as the standard Bombay Dyeing Confirmation. And paragraph 13, although more confusing than the standard form's language, differs only slightly. It read (once again, with all errors in the original):

> All dispute and question whatever which shall arise between the parties here o out of or as to the construetions of application there of or the resp ctive right and obtigation of the parties hereunder clause or thing here in contain or any account of valuarion to be made hereunder or as any ather matter in any way relating to these presents shall be referred to arbitration in accordance with the for the same beiag in force as applicable to piece goods for export and which will be framed by The Cotton Textile Export Promotion Council in consultation with the Mills nnd Exporters Representative selected in accordance with the provision therein Nothing in the rules or arbitration or any implication there of which runs counter ta the terms and conditions of this contrace applied sher to.

4 James Pitts left Chelsea in May of 1997. Lazar and Gribetz are the only remaining principals at Chelsea.

Based on Bombay Dyeing's representations to James Pitts regarding its capacity, Chelsea in turn entered into an exclusive sales agreement with a retailer, Bed, Bath & Beyond ("BB & B"), under which Chelsea agreed to provide finished linen textile products, such as sheets, pillowcases and shams, to BB & B. These were to be supplied by Bombay Dyeing. The Chelsea Square plaintiffs contend that BB & B projected linen sales of between $3,500,000 to $7,000,000, stemming from the agreement.

> Why do you think that the court spends so much time giving all of this background information? Do you think that the relationship between the parties is legally significant?

B. *The Sales Confirmations and Arbitration Clauses at Issue*

After extensive negotiations between James Pitts and Bombay Dyeing, Chelsea sent purchase orders during the months of May, June, July and August of 1996 for goods with a total value of $458,055. According to plaintiffs' complaint, Bombay Dyeing accepted the orders in one of three ways: (1) by providing a formal, written Confirmation, (2) by providing informal, written confirmation through a responsive letter or fax transmission, or (3) by orally confirming its acceptance of the order. Bombay Dyeing contends that it responded to each purchase order by sending its standard Confirmation to Chelsea, several of which were received into evidence in original form at an evidentiary hearing held by the district court. The district court aptly described these Confirmations and the arbitration clause contained therein:

> Each of the Chelsea Confirmations is printed on translucent tissue style paper and bears a legend on the top of its face page which is identical to that found on the Wadia Confirmation . . . The Chelsea Confirmations also bear on the back page what appear to be twenty-two numbered paragraphs entitled "Conditions," including at Condition 13 an arbitration clause similar to that found in the Wadia Confirmation. The presentation ***293** of this clause . . . is obscured by several printing defects. First, and most confusingly, the Conditions are arranged in columns juxtaposed in reverse order so that Conditions 1–12 are printed in the second of the two columns, with Conditions 14 through 22 appearing in the first. Condition 13 straddles both columns in reverse order, so that it begins in the lower right hand corner of the page, and concludes in the upper left hand corner. Second, the majority of the Chelsea Confirmations submitted by Bombay bear a first column which is printed partially off the page. Third, the Conditions are printed in type which is so faint as to border on the ephemeral, a condition which is compounded by the

> translucent nature of the tissue paper itself. Fourth, the details of the particular articles ordered by Chelsea are typewritten in heavy capitalized characters on the thin tissue of each Chelsea Confirmation's face page, effectively obliterating in places the faintly written Conditions on the reverse side.

Notwithstanding the foregoing disparaging comments regarding the Confirmation's legibility, the district court was able to reproduce the text of paragraph 13 which turned out to be no more well-written than its predecessors. Paragraph 13 reads (once again, with all errors in the original):

> All dispute and question whatever which shall rise between the parties here out of or as to the construction or application thereof or the respective right and obligation of the parties hereunder clause or things here in contain or any account of valuation to be made hereunder or as any other matter in any way relating to these presents shall be referred to arbitration in accordance with the for the same being in force as applicable to piece goods for export and which will be framed by the Cotton Textile Export Promotion Council in consultation with the Mills & Exporter Representatives selected in accordance with the provision there in nothing in the rules or arbitration or any implication there of which runs counter to the terms of conditions of the contract shall be applied here to.

Nancy Pitts signed the front side of at least one of the Confirmations—that received by fax on May 5, 1996—and there is no dispute that the signed page bore the same legend found on all Bombay Dyeing Confirmations, namely "We hereby confirm having sold to you goods as detailed below on the terms and conditions as started (sic) herein and as printed overleaf." In an affidavit submitted to the district court, however, Nancy Pitts denied ever receiving or reading the reverse side of the form, and contended that she never had any discussions with Bombay Dyeing regarding arbitration as a means of dispute resolution. In fact, the Chelsea Square plaintiffs contend that no one at Chelsea ever saw the arbitration clauses at issue or discussed the possibility of arbitrating disputes with anyone from Bombay Dyeing.

> Do you think that it matters whether Nancy Pitts signed the Confirmations? Is signing them necessary for the provisions to become part of the contract?

C. *The Underlying Dispute*

The underlying dispute in this case involves claims by the Chelsea Square plaintiffs that Bombay Dyeing failed to perform satisfactorily under the various contracts between the parties. Specifically, plaintiffs contend that certain goods ordered from Bombay Dyeing in April, 1996, were delivered late, and that others did not conform to those ordered—for example, top sheets were shipped without matching bottom sheets or pillowcases. Bombay Dyeing responds that Chelsea failed to pay for goods it actually received, and that Bombay Dyeing refused to complete the order until Chelsea paid for those goods.

D. *Proceedings Below*

On September 30, 1997, the Chelsea Square plaintiffs informed Bombay Dyeing of their planned suit for breach of contract to recover lost profits arising from Bombay's failure to perform. In a response dated October 9, 1997, Bombay Dyeing informed Chelsea that it had initiated arbitration ***294** proceedings in India under the auspices of Texprocil pursuant to paragraph 13 of the contract between the parties. A week later, Texprocil confirmed arbitration proceedings had been initiated and called upon Chelsea to appoint an arbitrator in accordance with Texprocil's rules. By letter dated December 1, 1997, Chelsea replied that it had never agreed to arbitrate any disputes with Bombay Dyeing and that it would not participate in the arbitration proceedings.

On December 5, 1997, the Chelsea Square plaintiffs filed this action in the Southern District of New York, asserting claims for, among other things, breach of contract, fraud, and negligent misrepresentation. On February 24, 1998, Bombay Dyeing moved to dismiss or stay the action and to compel arbitration in India pursuant to 9 U.S.C. § 206, which provides that "[a] court having jurisdiction under this chapter may direct that arbitration be held in accordance with the agreement at any place therein provided for, whether that place is within or without the United States." Plaintiffs opposed the motion and filed a cross-motion on March 16, 1998, to enjoin Bombay Dyeing from participating in the Indian arbitration.

In an unpublished July 23, 1998 Memorandum and Decision, the district court refused to stay the action and compel arbitration and enjoined Bombay Dyeing from pursuing the Indian arbitration. The district court concluded that its findings that the arbitration clauses relied upon by Bombay Dyeing were, "if not entirely illegible, . . . virtually incomprehensible," had two consequences: (1) Chelsea's failure to understand the effect of the clauses was reasonable, and (2) Chelsea simply could not have assented to, or become bound by, those clauses as a matter of New York law. This interlocutory appeal followed.

On appeal, Bombay Dyeing contends that the district court erred in its analysis of New York law and, specifically, in its conclusion that the arbitration clause contained in the Confirmations was unenforceable because it was illegible and unintelligible. For the reasons that follow, we agree.

II. DISCUSSION

A. *Arbitration—General Principles Under the FAA*

The FAA was enacted to promote the enforcement of privately entered agreements to arbitrate, "according to their terms." *Mastrobuono v. Shearson Lehman Hutton, Inc.,* 514 U.S. 52, 54, 115 S.Ct. 1212, 131 L.Ed.2d 76 (1995) (internal citation and quotation marks omitted). Through the FAA, Congress has declared a "strong federal policy favoring arbitration as an alternative means of dispute resolution." *Oldroyd v. Elmira Sav. Bank, FSB,* 134 F.3d 72, 76 (2d Cir.1998). As a result, the Supreme Court has instructed that "any doubts concerning the scope of arbitrable issues should be resolved in favor of arbitration, whether the problem at hand is the construction of the contract language itself or an allegation of waiver, delay, or a like defense to arbitrability." *Moses H. Cone Mem'l Hosp. v. Mercury Constr. Corp.,* 460 U.S. 1, 24–25, 103 S.Ct. 927, 74 L.Ed.2d 765 (1983). This bias in favor of arbitration, "is even stronger in the context of international transactions." *Deloitte Noraudit A/S v. Deloitte Haskins & Sells, U.S.,* 9 F.3d 1060, 1063 (2d Cir.1993). In determining whether a particular dispute is arbitrable, a court must engage in a two-part inquiry: it must decide (1) whether the parties agreed to arbitrate, and if so, (2) whether the scope of that agreement encompasses the asserted claims. *See Campaniello Imports, Ltd. v. Saporiti Italia S.p.A.,* 117 F.3d 655, 666 (2d Cir.1997). This case turns almost entirely on the first part of the inquiry—to wit, whether Chelsea agreed to arbitrate pursuant to paragraph 13 on the reverse side of the Confirmations at issue.

* * *

C. *Agreement to Arbitrate—Application of State Law*

* * *

Plaintiffs do not, and cannot, dispute that Chelsea entered into a series of binding contracts with Bombay Dyeing for the purchase of textiles, irrespective of whether they or anyone employed at Chelsea actually read the terms and conditions printed on the reverse side of the Confirmations. In fact, at oral argument, plaintiffs' counsel went further, rightly conceding that if the arbitration clause found in paragraph 13 had been legible and clearly written, there is little question that plaintiffs would be bound to arbitrate their dispute with Bombay Dyeing. *See Level Export Corp. v. Wolz, Aiken & Co.,* 305 N.Y. 82, 87, 111 N.E.2d 218 (1953) (buyer could not avoid arbitration by claiming he was unaware of and never read arbitration provision incorporated in binding contract); *see also* N.Y. U.C.C. §§ 2–207(1)–(2) (written confirmation sent within reasonable time operates as acceptance even though it states additional terms; additional terms become part of contract between merchants unless they "materially alter" agreement, or notice of objection to additional terms is given within reasonable time); *Gaynor-Stafford Indus., Inc. v. Mafco Textured Fibers,* 52 A.D.2d 481, 384 N.Y.S.2d 788, 789–91 (App. Div., 1st Dep't 1976) (construing § 2–207 in context of agreement between textile merchants, and concluding that arbitration clause contained in written order acknowledgment did not "materially alter" agreement given custom and practice of arbitration in industry).

What does this tell you about the NYBC case? I think that Susan should read this *Level Export* case.

Susan should read this case too. It's important to get a sense of how the New York courts look at a wide range of these cases.

Nonetheless, the Chelsea Square plaintiffs contend that the district court rightly found that Bombay Dyeing had not established that Chelsea had agreed to arbitrate disputes with it, given the district court's finding that the clause was illegible and unintelligible. We disagree.

We accept the district court's factual finding that the arbitration clause at issue was nearly illegible given certain printing defects and the fact that the clause was printed on very thin, tissue-style paper, which resulted in some of the text being obscured by typing on the reverse side. Nonetheless, the district court was able to reproduce the clause's text, with all of its defects. And, although the text itself is indeed garbled, we disagree with the district court's legal conclusion that the clause was unintelligible to a business like Chelsea that was operated by an experienced textile merchant, James Pitts, who had been purchasing textiles from Bombay Dyeing pursuant to the same basic sales Confirmation form for approximately a decade. *See Leadertex, Inc. v. Morganton Dyeing & Finishing Corp.*, 67 F.3d 20, 25 (2d Cir.1995) (evidence of trade usage and course of dealings between parties supported district court's finding of an agreement to arbitrate). The front of each Confirmation plainly informed the textile buyer that any sale would be governed by the terms and conditions printed on the reverse side.

Susan needs to investigate this further. How does a court determine whether arbitration clauses are common in the trade or business at issue?

We believe that a textile buyer is generally on notice that an agreement to purchase textiles is not only likely, but almost certain, to contain a provision mandating arbitration in the event of disputes, and must object to such a provision if it seeks to avoid arbitration. *See Helen Whiting, Inc. v. Trojan Textile Corp.*, 307 N.Y. 360, 367, 121 N.E.2d 367 (1954) ("From our own experience, we can almost take judicial ***297** notice that arbitration clauses are commonly used in the textile industry . . . ."); *see also In re Gaynor-Stafford*, 384 N.Y.S.2d at 790–91; *Leadertex*, 67 F.3d at 25; *Pervel Indus., Inc. v. T M Wallcovering, Inc.*, 871 F.2d 7, 8 (2d Cir.1989) (holding that textile buyer was bound by purchase order confirmations containing an arbitration clause where buyer did not object to provision, in part on the ground that arbitration clauses are "widespread" in textile industry); *Imptex Int'l Corp. v. Lorprint, Inc.*, 625 F.Supp. 1572, 1572 (S.D.N.Y.1986) ("The New York courts have repeatedly held that, as arbitration clauses are commonly used in the textile trade, a textile buyer's failure to object to an arbitration clause upon receipt of both the sales agreement signed by the seller and the initial shipment of goods binds the buyer to the arbitration clause.").

Susan has a lot of reading to do. Each of these cases will help her to determine how NY courts evaluate these cases.

For these reasons, we hold that Chelsea was bound by the arbitration clause printed on the reverse side of the Bombay Dyeing Confirmations to which it did not object. Moreover, although the clause does not state that the arbitration is to take place in India, it does state that arbitration is to be conducted in accordance with rules "framed by The Cotton Textile Export Promotion Council [Texprocil]," which, in turn, mandate that the arbitration be held in Bombay, India.

CONCLUSION

Accordingly, we vacate the district court's stay of arbitration, reverse its decision denying Bombay-Dyeing's motion to stay the action and compel arbitration, and direct the parties to proceed to arbitration pursuant to the rules set forth by Texprocil in Bombay, India. Costs shall be borne by appellees.

4. USING LEGAL RESEARCH AND THE COMMON LAW ARGUMENT GUIDE TO WRITE A LEGAL MEMORANDUM

Based on these two cases, Susan will have learned quite a bit. First of all, it seems that the court was correct to focus on the *Aceros* and *Chelsea Textiles* cases. Each of them has a fact pattern that is similar to the NYBC case. By carefully reading those opinions, Susan can get a great start on learning the relevant law. In addition, the courts in those cases cited other cases that might help Susan. Susan will have to go online and find each of the opinions cited by the *Aceros* and *Chelsea Textiles* courts. Although the court did some explanation of the authorities that it cited, it does not have to explain its legal conclusions in the level of detail that Susan will have to.

Further, Susan must read all of the relevant law and try to figure out how courts generally approach these cases under UCC 2–207(2). She must think carefully about what other judges have said about different facts in different cases. Ultimately, she will want to articulate a theme that captures what the courts do when confronted with a case under UCC 2–207(2). Her job in writing the memo is not to write a report about the existing law, however. Her job is to explain what the courts are doing in a way that helps Maryanne to think specifically about the NYBC problem.

In the District Court opinion, the judge ruled on the issue of whether the parties had agreed to arbitrate their disputes. He concluded that the arbitration clause that the defendant, MWC, had included in its Confirmation became part of the parties' contract under NY UCC 2–207(2). Although the judge cited authorities to support his conclusion, he did not explain his ruling fully. That is, even though the judge ruled in MWC's favor, it is possible that NYBC could make a successful argument on appeal that the District Court judge made an error of law. The partner at the firm representing NYBC will ask an associate at the firm to evaluate the District Court opinion. The associate must carefully read all of the sources that the District Court cited, and she must also do additional legal research to see whether the District Court applied the law in accordance with precedent or whether NYBC might be able to successfully appeal the District Court ruling.

Associates at law firms address legal questions in a variety of ways depending upon what the partner asks. Sometimes a quick email will be sufficient. For example, in this case, a partner might ask an associate to simply verify that the District Court opinion is correct. The associate might do extensive legal research—both reading the cases cited in the opinion and researching other possibly relevant legal sources, and then the associate might write a quick email to the partner with his conclusions. Other times, however, a partner will want a fuller explanation of the law and a more precise analysis of how the relevant law applies to the facts of the case. In those situations, an associate will write a legal memorandum.

The partner will expect that the associate will cite all of the relevant law and that he will give full analyses of the most important legal sources. A good legal memorandum anticipates the partner's questions about the case and answers them fully. A good legal memorandum will make a clear conclusion, but it will also explain possible counter arguments to the writer's legal conclusions. A good legal memorandum (and a good law school exam) acknowledges that both sides of an argument might have some support; however, the writer will always have to explain why his chosen solution is more likely to win in court.

These writing challenges of the associate in a legal memorandum are very different from those of the judge in the legal opinion. The judge must simply decide the case and offer some authority for his conclusions. His main job is to decide the case. Often judges do not give much legal analysis of the cases that they rely on. Similarly, judges might not offer any analysis of counter arguments. Again, the judge's job is to decide the case. Some judges, especially Justices of the Supreme Court, do give extensive analysis of the law, including possible counter-arguments; however, many lower court judges do not.

As you read Susan's legal memorandum about the *NYBC v. MWC* case, try to notice how this document is different from the legal opinions on the same topic. Further, try to determine whether you think that Susan has fully satisfied Maryanne's expectations for the legal analysis of the relevant law. Please refer to the Common Law Argument Guide, reproduced below, to help you to evaluate the legal arguments in Susan's memorandum.

Common Law Argument Guide

Whenever you are reading U.S. common law legal arguments in any form of U.S. Legal English-cases; law review articles; legal memorandums, you must evaluate the writer's common law arguments. The writer should make it easy for you to see how his legal conclusions are supported by the legal sources that he discusses and cites. That is, you must evaluate whether the writer has given you enough information in order to determine whether his common law arguments are successful and convincing. As you read U.S. common law arguments, try to focus on the following things:

1) **Precedent.** Think about how the writer has chosen the statutes and cases that are being used to support his legal conclusions. Are they from the appropriate jurisdiction? Are they state law or are they federal law? Are the cases from the highest court in the jurisdiction or from a lower court?

2) **Analogy.** Think about how the writer has used the legally significant facts in the cases that are cited. Has he explained how the legally significant facts in these cases are either similar to or different from the facts of the case that the writer is discussing?

3) **Legal Issue(s).** Think about the primary legal issues that the writer is addressing. Are these legal issues the same as those in the cases that the writer is citing? How are they the same or different?

4) **Legal Reasoning.** Think about the rationale the courts used in deciding the cited cases that the writer is discussing; that is, has the writer explained how each court applied the law to the facts in each case?

5) **Legal Conclusions.** Think about the writer's legal conclusions on the points that he is addressing. Has the writer convinced you that his legal conclusions are supported by the applicable law?

As you read Susan's memorandum, try to take notes and try to write down your evaluation of the memorandum using the Common Law Argument Guide.

A. SUSAN'S LEGAL MEMORANDUM ON THE *NYBC V. MWC* CASE

Memorandum

To: Maryanne Blackmun, Partner

From: Susan Cooke, Senior Associate

Re: New York Box Company v. Manhattan Watch Company

Facts

Our client, NYBC, filed a suit for non-payment against MWC in the U.S. District Court for the Southern District of New York.[3] The judge granted the defendant's motion to dismiss the case on grounds that the parties had agreed to arbitrate all disputes under the contract. NYBC contends that it never agreed to arbitrate, and it would like to appeal the court's ruling.

> It is customary to begin a legal discussion about a possible appeal of a lower court ruling by summarizing the procedural history of the case.

NYBC entered into a contract with MWC through a series of negotiations and subsequent exchanges of confirming emails and documents. It is undisputed that the parties agreed to an initial three-year contract under which NYBC would ship 10,000 boxes to MWC each month at a cost of $10 per box. The boxes were to be made to MWC's specifications. NYBC would send invoices to MWC with each shipment. Payment was due by the 15th of the month.

> These facts prepare the reader to understand the reasoning in the cases cited in the memorandum. The cases discuss how parties make contracts using emails and other communications.

Each time that MWC received a shipment of boxes from NYBC, it sent to NYBC a Confirmation, which verified that the shipped boxes conformed to MWC's specifications and that they were delivered on time. On the back of these Confirmations, MWC included an explicit arbitration clause, which stated that the parties agreed to arbitrate all disputes under the contract in New York.

Shortly after NYBC sent its first shipment of boxes to MWC, and after MWC sent its first Confirmation to NYBC, the CEO of MWC called the CEO of NYBC to ask whether everything was OK. NYBC's CEO responded that everything was fine. After about a year, however, MWC began complaining to NYBC that the boxes were no longer satisfactory. NYBC responded that the boxes were exactly the same as they had always been. Ultimately, even though NYBC continued to ship boxes to MWC in accordance with their three-year contract, MWC stopped paying NYBC's invoices. NYBC filed suit in federal district court for breach of contract and for non-payment.

[3] Because NYBC is a New York corporation, and MWC is a Delaware corporation, the federal district court had diversity jurisdiction in this case. Because all events in this case took place in the State of New York, the court determined that New York law applies to this contract dispute between the parties.

In response to NYBC's lawsuit, MWC filed a motion for the court to dismiss the suit because the parties had agreed to arbitrate, based on the arbitration clause contained in the Confirmations. The district court agreed. The court dismissed the suit and ordered the parties to arbitrate. The client, NYBC, would like to appeal the District Court's ruling to the Second Circuit Court of Appeals.

Discussion

The arbitration clause contained in MWC's Confirmation is likely to become part of the parties' contract under NY UCC 2–207, and a Second Circuit Court of Appeals is likely to uphold the District Court's order to compel the parties to arbitrate their dispute because the arbitration clause will not materially alter their contract. The Court is likely to base its ruling on New York state and federal court interpretations of the Federal Arbitration Act (FAA) and of NY UCC 2–207. We should advise NYBC not to appeal the District Court's ruling and to proceed to arbitrate its claims against MWC.

> Susan begins the Discussion with the legal conclusion. This initial paragraph serves as a "roadmap" to the Discussion section.

The FAA States a Strong Preference for Arbitration.

> This section gives some background for understanding the New York law.

Although a court must apply principles of state law to decide whether the parties agreed to arbitrate their dispute, the Federal Arbitration Act (FAA) has been interpreted to establish a "liberal federal policy favoring arbitration agreements." *Moses H. Cone Memorial Hospital v. Mercury Construction Corp.,* 460 U.S. 1, 24 (1983). The U.S. Supreme Court has also observed that, "[t]he preeminent concern of Congress in passing the Act was to enforce private agreements into which parties had entered," a concern which "requires that we rigorously enforce agreements to arbitrate." *Dean Witter Reynolds Inc. v. Byrd,* 470 U.S. 213, 221 (1985).

Further, the Supreme Court has also said "that questions of arbitrability must be addressed with a healthy regard for the federal policy favoring arbitration. . . . The Arbitration Act establishes that, as a matter of federal law, any doubts concerning the scope of arbitrable issues should be resolved in favor of arbitration, whether the problem at hand is the construction of the contract language itself or an allegation of waiver, delay, or a like defense to arbitrability. *Moses H. Cone Memorial Hospital v. Mercury Construction Corp.*, 460 U.S. 24–25.

NY UCC 2-207 States a Strong Preference for the Inclusion of Additional Terms in Contracts Between Merchants.

This heading, and all headings in the Discussion, makes a clear legal conclusion that helps the reader to understand the case.

NY UCC 2–207 addresses the situation between MWC and NYBC. The entire text of the statute appears below:

§ 2–207. Additional Terms in Acceptance or Confirmation

(1) A definite and seasonable expression of acceptance or a written confirmation which is sent within a reasonable time operates as an acceptance even though it states terms additional to or different from those offered or agreed upon, unless acceptance is expressly made conditional on assent to the additional or different terms.

(2) The additional terms are to be construed as proposals for addition to the contract. Between merchants such terms become part of the contract unless:

When discussing statutory law, it is important to quote the words of the statute.

a. the offer expressly limits acceptance to the terms of the offer;

b. they materially alter it; or

c. notification of objection to them has already been given or is given within a reasonable time after notice of them is received.

(3) Conduct by both parties which recognizes the existence of a contract is sufficient to establish a contract for sale although the writings of the parties do not otherwise establish a contract. In such case the terms of the particular contract consist of those terms on which the writings of the parties agree, together with any supplementary terms incorporated under any other provisions of this Act.

In the *NYBC v. MWC* case, neither of the parties disputes that they had created a three-year contract through their oral agreements and through their subsequent written email exchange. Whether the parties had a contract before MWC sent its first Confirmation including the arbitration clause is not in dispute. The issue here is simply whether the "additional terms" included in the Confirmation became part of this contract under UCC 2–207(2).

In this paragraph, Susan explains which part of 2–207 will be relevant to this case.

Section (1) addresses the issue of whether and under what conditions additional terms can become part of a contract. New York courts and federal courts interpreting New York law have repeatedly interpreted UCC 2–207(1) to incorporate additional terms even where one of the parties was not explicitly aware of them. For example, in *Ronan Associates, Inc. v. Local 94–94A,* the Second Circuit, applying New York law, ruled that parties were obligated to arbitrate their disputes under an arbitration clause that they never signed when that clause was incorporated by reference from other documents. *Ronan Associates, Inc. v. Local 94–94A,* 24 F.3d 447, 449 (2d Cir. 1994). This has been the long-standing interpretation of UCC 2–207. *See Level Export Corp. v. Wolz, Aiken & Co.,* 305 NY 82, 87 (1953) (ruling that a party could not avoid arbitration by claiming that he was unaware of an arbitration clause incorporated into a binding contract).

Further, New York courts have specifically ruled that the party objecting to the arbitration clause does not need to have read the arbitration clause in order to be bound by it, if it is properly incorporated by reference under UCC 2–207. In *Aceros v. Tradearbed,* the Second Circuit, again applying New York law, ruled that an arbitration clause on the back of a purchase order would be incorporated into the parties' contract even though the objecting party had not read it. *Aceros Prefabricados, S.A. v. Tradearbed, Inc.,* 282 F.3d 97 (2002).

Also, in *Chelsea Textiles v. Bombay Dying,* the court ruled that a disputed arbitration clause would become part of the parties' contract even though it was badly written and difficult to see. *Chelsea Textiles v. Bombay Dyeing,* 189 F.3d 289 (2nd Cir. 1999). In that case, the arbitration clause was written on very thin paper in very light type. The party objecting to the clause argued that its illegibility prevented it from being included in the contract. The court ruled however that the arbitration clause was incorporated into the contract and it was up to the parties to familiarize themselves with it. *Chelsea Textiles* at 293.

NY UCC 2–207 Imposes Greater Burdens on Merchants.

The NY law in UCC 2–207(2) focuses specifically on contracts between merchants. In interpreting this section, the courts have understood that merchants often create contracts using multiple documents over a period of time. At some point, when the parties have agreed in writing on the essential terms of their contract—price; quantity; and duration of the contract, they have a deal. If documents, such as the Confirmation that MWC sent to NYBC, arrive after the parties have concluded the contract, those additional terms will become part of the contract if they meet the criteria in UCC 2–207(2).

In the case of a contract between two merchants,[4] the court will focus on whether the inclusion of the additional terms will "materially alter" the parties' contract.

NYBC Must Show That the Arbitration Clause Would Materially Alter the Contract in This Case.

Under section 2–207(2), any proposed additional terms will become part of the contract between merchants unless one of the three statutory exceptions is satisfied: 1) the offer expressly limits acceptance to the terms of the offer; 2) the additional term will materially alter the contract; or 3) notification of objection to the additional term has already been given or is given within a reasonable time after notice of the new term is received. In the *NYBC v. MWC* situation, subsections (1) and (3) seem to be irrelevant. MWC did not require an affirmative acceptance of the additional terms, and NYBC did not specifically object to them.

The only issue to be resolved is whether the addition of the arbitration clause materially altered the contract between NYBC and MWC. The New York courts have a long line of cases discussing what constitutes a material alteration to a contract. Overall, the decision depends upon the degree to which the additional term would be a surprise or a hardship to the party that is objecting to it.

Because UCC 2–207(2) assumes that, between merchants, the additional terms will be included, the burden is on the party objecting to the additional terms to prove that the addition of these terms would be a material alteration to the contract. *See, e.g. Bayway Refining Co. v. Oxygenated Marketing and Trading A.G.,* 215 F.3d 219, 223 (2nd Cir. 2000) (applying NY law); *JOM, Inc. v. Adell Plastics, Inc.,* 193 F.3d 47, 59 (1st Cir. 1999) (discussing UCC 2–207 as applied in several jurisdictions); and Avedon Engineering Inc. v. Seatex, 126 F.3d 1279, 1284 (10th Cir. 1997)(applying NY law). *See also LTV Energy Prods. Co. v. Northern States Contracting Co. (In re Chateaugay Corp.),* 162 B.R. 949, 952, 957–58 (Bankr.S.D.N.Y.1994) (summarizing recent case law supporting the proposition that the party objecting to the additional term must prove that the additional term was a "material alteration").

A material alteration is one that would "result in *surprise* or *hardship* if incorporated without express awareness by the other party." *See N.Y. U.C.C. section 2–207 cmt. 4, Id.* at 224. Surprise, within the meaning of the material alternation exception of section 2–207(2)(b), has both a subjective element of what a party actually knew and an objective element of what a party should have known. *See American Ins. Co. v. El Paso Pipe and Supply Co.,* 978 F.2d 1185 (10th Cir. 1992) (applying New Mexico law, but citing cases from several jurisdictions applying UCC 2–207); *In re Chateaugay Corp.,* 162 B.R. 949, 957 (Bankr.S.D.N.Y. 1994).

To carry the burden of showing surprise, a party must establish that it cannot be presumed that a reasonable merchant would have consented to the additional term.

---

[4] NY UCC 2–104(1): "Merchant" means a person who deals in goods of the kind or otherwise by his occupation holds himself out as having knowledge or skill peculiar to the practices or goods involved in the transaction or to whom such knowledge or skill may be attributed by his employment of an agent or broker or other intermediary who by his occupation holds himself out as having such knowledge or skill.

See Bayway Refining Co., 215 F.3d at 224. (quoting *Union Carbide Corp.,* 947 F.2d 1336.)

The court in *Aceros Prefabricados, S.A.* concluded that Aceros had not met its burden of proving "surprise." The court found that the parties had never explicitly discussed arbitration and Aceros testified that it did not know about the arbitration clause until the lawsuit was filed. Nonetheless, Aceros had failed to show objective surprise. The court ruled that, in this case, the arbitration clause should have been expected by merchants in this business, and the addition of the arbitration clause was not a material alteration of the contract. 282 F.3d at 101. The opposing party has the burden of *establishing* the elements of surprise, not merely stating that they are present. *Id.*

NYBC's CEO has stated that he was in a great shock when he discovered that there was an arbitration clause on the back of the Confirmations. In fact, he didn't even know that MWC had sent Confirmations with its payments to NYBC. Although this might demonstrate a subjective surprise, it does not constitute evidence that a reasonable merchant in a similar position would have been objectively surprised by the arbitration clause.

NYBC Must Show That Arbitration Is Not Standard Practice in This Industry.

Courts will generally deny a party's claim of surprise for the purposes of UCC 2–207(2) if arbitration is a standard practice in the relevant industry. *Chelsea Textiles,* at 289. The court will review evidence submitted by the parties about standard trade and usage in the relevant industry. NY courts have found that arbitration clauses are part of standard trade and usage in a wide variety of industries. *See e.g. Chelsea Textiles,* 189 F.3rd at 293 (finding that arbitration clauses are standard in the textile industry); *Aceros* at 104 (also finding that arbitration clauses are standard in the textile industry); *Bayway Refining,* 215 F. 3rd at 225 (finding that arbitration clauses are standard in the petroleum industry); Section 3-3, James J. White and Robert S. Summers, *Uniform Commercial Code,* West (Fifth Ed. 2000) (surveying industries where arbitration clauses are part of standard industry trade and practice).

It is unlikely that NYBC could provide evidence to support a claim that arbitration is not part of the standard trade and usage in the box manufacturing industry. Rather, it is likely that a NY court would find that the box industry is not unique and that the addition of an arbitration clauses to the parties' contract would not be a material alteration to the contract.

Conclusion: The Court of Appeals for the 2nd Circuit Is Likely to Uphold the Decision of the Federal District Court to Dismiss the Case and to Order Arbitration.

Because the parties are merchants, and because it is unlikely that NYBC could provide evidence that the addition of an arbitration clause would be a material alteration to the contract, it is likely that the arbitration clause is part of the parties' contract. It is therefore unlikely that NYBC would win its appeal of the Federal District Court's ruling to order the parties to arbitrate their dispute.

CHAPTER 4

MEETING THE EXPECTATIONS OF THE LEGAL READER: COMPARING TWO LEGAL ANALYSES OF THE SAME LEGAL PROBLEM

■ ■ ■

1. INTRODUCTION

So far, in Chapter 1, you have observed while Maria and her colleagues wrote legal analyses of two fairly simple legal problems under the fictitious law of New Columbia. In Chapter 2, you observed as three Justices of the U.S. Supreme Court analyzed very complex U.S. Constitutional issues in the majority, dissent, and concurrence opinions in the case of *Erie v. Tompkins.* In Chapter 3, you have observed how a U.S. law firm associate wrote a legal analysis of a statutory problem under New York law. In all of these situations, you have used the Common Law Argument Guide to help you to understand how U.S. lawyers make and evaluate common law legal arguments.

In this Chapter, you will have the opportunity to use the analytic skills that you have learned in the previous Chapters to analyze legal arguments concerning a very complex legal problem involving a common law doctrine of New York contract law: *the implied covenant of good faith and fair dealing.* Although it is unlikely that you have any experience with this doctrine of New York law, you will see that you are very prepared to criticize the legal arguments made by the writers of the legal analyses that you will read.

Being able to criticize common law arguments that other lawyers write is the best way to prepare to write legal arguments of your own. As you read these legal arguments, think about the Common Law Argument Guide—reproduced here.

Common Law Argument Guide

Whenever you are reading U.S. common law legal arguments in any form of U.S. Legal English-cases; law review articles; legal memorandums, you must evaluate the writer's common law arguments. The writer should make it easy for you to see how his legal conclusions are supported by the legal sources that he discusses and cites. That is, you must evaluate whether the writer has given you enough information in order to determine whether his common law arguments are successful and convincing. As you read U.S. common law arguments, try to focus on the following things:

1) **Precedent.** Think about how the writer has chosen the statutes and cases that are being used to support his legal conclusions. Are they from the appropriate jurisdiction? Are they state law or are they federal law? Are the cases from the highest court in the jurisdiction or from a lower court?

2) **Analogy.** Think about how the writer has used the legally significant facts in the cases that are cited. Has he explained how the legally significant facts in these cases are either similar to or different from the facts of the case that the writer is discussing?

3) **Legal Issue(s).** Think about the primary legal issues that the writer is addressing. Are these legal issues the same as those in the cases that the writer is citing? How are they the same or different?

4) **Legal Reasoning.** Think about the rationale the courts used in deciding the cited cases that the writer is discussing; that is, has the writer explained how each court applied the law to the facts in each case?

5) **Legal Conclusions.** Think about the writer's legal conclusions on the points that he is addressing. Has the writer convinced you that his legal conclusions are supported by the applicable law?

As you read the two legal memorandums that follow, ask yourself whether each of the writers has given you enough information about the cases that he is citing for you to understand his legal arguments. Has the writer provided enough legal support for his arguments? In U.S. legal practice, lawyers use Legal English in writing many kinds of documents: emails to clients and other lawyers; briefs to courts; responses to inquiries from potential clients; comments on pending administrative regulations. In all of these documents, U.S. lawyers use the same kind of reasoning. That is, they base their legal conclusions on precedent and by making analogies to other similar cases. You can use the Common Law Argument

Guide not only to evaluate the legal arguments that other lawyers make but also to help you to make successful legal arguments of your own.

Although lawyers in practice today do much of their legal analysis in the form of short emails to the lawyers they work with, sometimes lawyers must treat an issue with a more thorough approach. When an issue is important to the client and to the firm, a lawyer might draft a full legal memorandum, similar to the one that you will evaluate in this Chapter. Susan produced a legal memorandum for Maryanne about the application of NY UCC 2–207 in Chapter 3. The legal memorandums in this Chapter provide the information needed to determine how to advise the client. Law partners are always very busy people, with many cases to consider and many business lunches to attend. Often, the partner relies on the junior associate to provide an analysis of the client's case, in the form of a legal memorandum, which relies on careful consideration of the legal theories that pertain to the client's case. A successful legal memorandum does much more than to simply provide quoted language from previous cases. A valuable and successful legal memorandum must apply case law and common law argumentation to the facts of the client's case. In this Chapter, you will learn about the kind of information and argumentation that is found in a complex legal memorandum.

An excellent way to become familiar with conventions and preferred patterns of an unfamiliar area of the law is to closely read successful (and not so successful) documents that would be valued by members of the U.S. legal community. In this Chapter, you will see two examples of a legal memorandum which addresses the issue of the New York contract law doctrine of good faith and fair dealing. Accompanying each memorandum is rather extensive commentary, which is meant to draw your attention to three aspects of the writing—the common law argumentation (as expressed in the Common Law Argument Guide), the overall structure of the memorandum, and various language strategies that make the writing more accessible to U.S. legal readers. All of this is what we refer to as Legal English.

The primary audience for the memorandum that we will look at in this Chapter is the partner who assigned it, and possibly other lawyers at the firm who are not familiar with the case. It is not likely that the client himself will read it. The legal memorandum is a document written by a lawyer for a legal audience. It is intended to assist the law firm in deciding how to advise the client. Because lawyers at the firm who are not involved in this case directly might read this memorandum when thinking about a future case with similar facts, you may not assume that all readers of the memorandum are knowledgeable either about the facts of the case or about the basics of the applicable laws. Rather, you must assume that those who are less familiar with both the facts and the case law are potential readers. This means you have a quite different audience to consider from the judge who writes the court's opinions. The judge is directing his opinion primarily to the parties in the case and to the lawyers who represent them. Consequently, the associate who is writing the legal memorandum often has to provide more complete analyses of prior cases and more explicit, full common law argumentation in the legal memorandum than the judge does in his opinion. As we have seen in the case of *Erie v. Tompkins*, judges do sometimes write more explanatory opinions; however, U.S. lawyers who write legal memorandums must always fully explain their legal arguments.

The legal memorandum typically begins with an overview of the facts of the case. As you will recall from Chapter 3, this overview focuses on what we call the "legally significant facts." That is, the lawyer must first understand the applicable law and identify the kinds of facts that courts rely on when making their decisions in cases involving the law. Of course, the writer will also include some background facts that will help the reader to understand the factual context; however, the structure of the fact section of the legal memorandum should prepare the reader for the legal arguments that follow in the legal discussion. The best way to do that is to structure the facts section around the law. As we analyze the sample memorandums in this Chapter, try to evaluate whether you think that the fact sections sufficiently prepare the reader for the legal analysis. Good lawyers always write the fact section last. A good writer knows that structure of the fact section depends on the law.

The next section of the memorandum is a statement of the legal questions raised by the client's case. The legal questions arise from your thoughtful analysis of applicable case law in relation to the facts in the client's case; they also provide an overall organization for the discussion in the body of the memorandum. As you will recall from the very simple analysis of the New Columbia "one free bite rule" in Chapter 1, Maria's colleague, Juan Carlos, began his legal discussion with a very helpful Roadmap paragraph based on the two-part test of the New Columbia common law rule.

In the type of formal legal memorandum that we will be looking at here, lawyers often include a separate section called Questions Presented/Brief Answers. This section tells the reader which issues will be discussed in the legal discussion, and it also briefly summarizes the legal conclusions.

The goal of the legal discussion section is to advise the partner on the likely outcome of pursuing the proposed legal strategies. It is important that the legal memorandum addresses possible problems with or counterarguments to the proposed strategies. Finally, the associate gives his or her best estimate as to the likely success of the proposed strategies.

When presenting a common law argument to support a legal conclusion, successful U.S. lawyers typically incorporate all of the parts of the Common Law Argument Guide. You can use the Common Law Argument Guide to help you to evaluate whether each lawyer's argument here is successful.

2. TEXTUAL ANALYSIS OF TWO LEGAL MEMORANDUMS

The commentary provided is meant to act as a guided tour of the content and form of the legal memorandum. A successful U.S. legal memorandum weaves together aspects of content and form to create a well-organized, well-articulated presentation of the client's case and the pertinent law. One purpose of taking you through this detailed tour of the legal memorandum is to make you more aware of how common law arguments can be successfully developed; this is the primary content of the legal memorandum.

Another purpose of the commentary is to make you more aware of successful Legal English writing strategies that you can use to make your legal arguments more precise and easier for the reader to follow. In other words, the commentary will help you to focus on the two types of Legal English that we discussed in Chapter 1: 1) English Grammar and Usage; and 2) Common Law Argumentation. As you read the memorandums and the accompanying commentary, try to read like as a U.S. lawyer, reading for information, but also to read like a U.S. legal writer so that you can become more aware of the variety of techniques and strategies successful writers use in creating effective common law arguments using Legal English.

A. SAMPLE MEMORANDUM I

Legal Memorandum

To: Partner

From: Associate

Re: Urbania's Sovereign Debt Restructuring

I. INTRODUCTION

Urbania's Ministry of Finance came to our office to describe a plan to restructure the country's sovereign debt through a bond exchange offer, using the so-called "exit amendment." This technique involves a possibility of rejection by some bondholders and, therefore, a litigation threat for Urbania. In principle, the "holdout" creditors could jeopardize the restructuring and, for this

> This paragraph quickly reminds the partner what this case was about and why it is important.

reason, Urbania asked our legal opinion on the risks involved.

The first part of this memorandum briefly outlines the relevant facts of the proposed restructuring, in accordance with Urbania's Ministry of Finance. The second part states the legal issue, which in this case involves the application of the good faith and fair dealing doctrine under the state of New York contract law. The following part discusses the relevant legal cases, and is divided in the following sections: (a) the issue of legal jurisdiction and immunity, considering that Urbania, as a foreign state, could be part of a conflict involving its Bond Agreement; (b) the modification clause of the contract, according to which the majority of bondholders can delete the tax gross up clause; (c) the concept of the good faith and fair dealing, more specifically in which context the courts have been applying it. In this section, we will review relevant cases to support our conclusion. The last part concludes that, considering the facts of Urbania's restructuring in connection with the legal cases analyzed, it is unlikely that the minority bondholders would succeed in a claim against Urbania for violation of the implied covenant of good faith and fair dealing.

> This is an excellent Roadmap paragraph. It prepares the reader for the organization of the text that follows, and it gives a clear legal conclusion. The writer, however, seems to assume that the reader knows many things about this case that he does not explain. What kind of bond agreement is involved here? What is a restructuring? What is a modification clause? The writer here needs to explain more about the context of this legal problem.

II. STATEMENT OF FACTS

Urbania issued sovereign bonds governed by New York contract law in the amount of $750,000,000 that will mature by the end of this calendar year. The country is going through a severe financial crisis and will not be able to pay its creditors on time. To avoid default, Urbania is considering a plan to restructure its debt through a bond exchange offer, using the so-called "exit amendment." In order to make the old bonds unattractive to the minority bondholders and motivate them to accept the exchange and the new bonds, the majority bondholders would vote to delete the tax gross up clause of the existing Bond Agreement.

> What is an "exchange offer"? What is an "exit amendment"? The writer needs to explain these terms to the reader.

According to Urbania's Ministry of Finance, 78% of bondholders are willing to agree with the restructuring plan. By allowing the majority bondholders to amend the contract, Urbania wishes to encourage the "holdout" creditors to participate in the exchange offer. The agreement's modification clause allows the deletion of the tax gross up clause with the written consent of 51% of the bondholders. As to the new bonds, Urbania would (a) change the face value of the bond from $1000 to $450; (b) extend the maturity date; (c) add a higher interest rate; and (d) keep the tax gross up clause.

> What is a tax gross-up clause? What is a modification clause? What is the exact language of the modification clause?

Urbania is aware of the litigation risk if adherence to the exchange is not 100% and needs a legal assessment of such risk. The country understands that the minority bondholders do not have a cause of action for breach of contract because the modification clause allows the majority bondholders to delete the tax gross up clause. However, since under New York law every contract contains an implied covenant of good faith and fair dealing, they are aware of the possibility of litigation and would like our analysis on similar cases where the covenant was applied. In other words, Urbania wants our legal opinion on the likelihood that the "holdout" creditors can effectively undermine the proposed exit amendment alleging that the deletion of the tax gross up clause, in the context of the exchange offer, violates any duties of good faith and fair dealing under the terms of the Bond Agreement.

III. LEGAL ISSUE

Under New York contract law, does the deletion of the tax gross up clause, in the context of the exchange offer proposed by Urbania, deprive the minority bondholders of the benefit of their bargain, thus violating the implied covenant of good faith and fair dealing?

> This statement of the legal question focuses on the main concerns of the legal reader: 1) it identifies the relevant law; 2) it incorporates the significant legal facts in the analysis; and 3) it identifies the legal test that courts use to evaluate these claims.

No. As we will see below in the analysis of relevant cases, it is not likely that the courts would conclude that Urbania violated any duties of good faith and fair dealing associated with the exchange offer. The courts tend to avoid implying a substantive right that was not considered by the parties on the date of their agreement. Furthermore, the courts would probably consider Urbania's financial situation and that the alternative to the exchange offer would be the country's default.

> This is a very useful summary of the reasons that the writer came to his legal conclusion. He has alerted the reader of the reasons that he does not believe that Urbania would be liable under the Good Faith and Fair Dealing doctrine. The reader is now aware of what to look for in the following text.

IV. LEGAL DISCUSSION

a) The issue of legal jurisdiction and immunity

The Bond Agreement determines that the contract shall be governed by New York law. Because Urbania is a sovereign state, the first issue we should focus on is legal jurisdiction. In other words, we should determine whether a court in the United States of America would have jurisdiction over Urbania. The Foreign Sovereign Immunities Act of 1976 (FSIA), 28 U.S.C.A. establishes that a foreign state is not immune for an action which is based upon a "commercial activity." In a similar case to the Urbania case, a sovereign country, Argentina, that issued bonds in the international market decided to reschedule the maturity date of the bonds (*Republic of Argentina and Banco Central v. Weltover, Inc.,* 504 U.S. 607 (1992)). Argentina was sued by the bondholders that did not agree with the rescheduling. In this particular case, Argentina argued that it was immune from the jurisdiction of the United States District Court for Southern District of New York, but the Supreme Court decided that the issuance of bonds was a "commercial activity" under FSIA, and therefore the U.S. had jurisdiction to take the case. In our case, it is most likely that the United States courts would exercise jurisdiction over Urbania if the minority bondholders decide to take action against the country.

> It is usually more helpful to the reader if these section headings make clear legal conclusions. For example, the writer might have said the following: "The Federal Court has Jurisdiction to Decide this Case Involving a Sovereign Government." Or he could have said something like this: "The Foreign Sovereign Immunities Act does not Protect Sovereigns When they Engage In Commercial Behavior."

> Although this section concludes that it is likely that a US court would take jurisdiction of the Urbania case, based on a comparison to the Argentinian case, do you think that the writer makes the case as clearly as possible? Do you think that a legal reader might have wanted to see more of the actual statutory language of the Foreign Sovereign Immunities Act? In most similar situations, a writer might put the entire relevant portion of the statutory language in a footnote so that the reader can see it. Would you find that to be helpful?

b) The modification clause of the Bond Agreement

The modification clause in Urbania's Bond Agreement authorizes the deletion of the tax gross up clause with the written consent of 51% of the bondholders. Accordingly, the clause only requires the consent of all bondholders if the modification would change the terms of currency of payment of the principal amount or interest on any bond or the amounts thereof. That is to say the modification clause does not mention the tax gross up clause. Consequently, if there is no specific provision in the modification clause about the tax gross up clause, and the principal amount is not going to change as a result of the deletion, the consent of

> Again, do you think that a reader might want to see the actual language from the Bond Clauses? Would you put that text in the body of the discussion or in a footnote? How would you decide?

all bondholders would not be required in Urbania's case. In *Sharon Steel Corp. v. Chase Manhattan Bank, N.A.,* 691 F. 2d 1039 (2d Cir. 1982), the Court applied New York law and held that "boiler-plate" provisions, such as payment terms in Yankee bonds (such as Urbania's) should be narrowly interpreted. For that reason, the courts are not likely to add any provisions to a Yankee bond that were not expressly agreed by the parties.

> Although the writer has identified a relevant case for comparison to the Urbania case (Step 1 in the Common Law Argument Guide), do you think that he has sufficiently explained the facts of that case or given the rationale of the court in that case (Steps 2 and 3 of the Common Law Argument Guide)?

For the reasons mentioned above, it is fair to assume that the minority bondholders would not sue Urbania for breach of contract. It is most likely that they would argue that the entire restructuring, meaning the deletion of the tax clause and the exchange offer, deprives them of the benefit of their bargain in a broader way. To put it another way, in case they decide to sue Urbania, they would probably take advantage of the good faith and fair dealing principle to argue that Urbania's real intention with the bond restructuring is not to avoid default but simply to cut out their profits. Also, the minority bondholders could argue that, because they had an expectation in relation to their profits, that was affected by the restructuring, and therefore Urbania violated the implied covenant of good faith and fair dealing. In view of that, for now on we will be focusing our analysis on the application of the good faith and fair dealing concept under the state of New York contract law.

> In this paragraph, the writer is making a distinction between a possible suit for breach of contract and a breach of the common law doctrine of good faith and fair dealing. Has the writer made that distinction clearly enough?
>
> Could you offer some suggestion of how this writer could have made this distinction more effectively? For example, could the writer have used parallel structure to more clearly point out the similarities and differences between these suits? Or, do you think that the sentences in this paragraph are just too long and complicated? If you have to say "To put it another way," maybe the first way that you said it was not very clear. ☺

c) The good faith and fair dealing doctrine and its application by the courts

Under New York law, every contract contains an implied covenant of good faith and fair dealing. The general idea of the principle is to preserve the reasonable expectations of the parties, and this concept was most useful in the past when the parties in a commercial contract did not have the assistance of counsels. In our time, especially in contracts such as Urbania's bond agreement, the parties are commercially sophisticated and they usually have experienced lawyers defending their interests.

> These two sentences contain clear legal conclusions. A legal reader would want to have citations to authority for each of them.

In *Reiss v. Financial Performance Corp.,* 97 N.Y. 2d 195 (2001), the Court found that the covenant of good faith and fair dealing cannot become an excuse for commercially sophisticated parties not to carefully address all relevant issues in their contract. In *Hartford Fire Insurance Co. v. Federated Department Stores, Inc.,* 723 F.Supp. 976, 991 (1989), applying New York law, the Court decided that "the implied covenant of good faith and fair dealing does not provide a court *carte blanche* to rewrite the parties' agreement. Thus, a court cannot imply a covenant inconsistent with terms expressly set forth in the contract" (citing *Gardner & Florence Call Cowles Found. v. Empire, Inc.,* 589 F.Supp. 669, 673 (1984)).

In short, it is fair to assume that nowadays the courts do not look like they have to protect the parties in a commercial relationship. In fact, they are reticent to apply the good faith and fair dealing doctrine and tend to avoid implying a right or adding a provision that was not agreed by the parties.

> Although this paragraph's conclusion might follow from the two cases just cited, the writer has not sufficiently fulfilled Steps 2 and 3 in the Common Law Argument Guide. I might need to re-read the cited cases—and that would make me an unhappy legal reader.

Nevertheless, in some cases the courts still apply the implied covenant of good faith and fair dealing. In *Van Gemert v. Boeing Co.,* 520 F.2d 1373 (1975), Boeing gave insufficient notice of redemption to debenture holders. The court, applying New York law, decided that the debenture holder's reasonable expectation as to notice should be protected. According to the court's reasoning, the debenture holder expects that the stock will increase sufficiently in value and that the conversion right will make the debenture worth more than the debt. Consequently, the debenture holder relies on the opportunity to make a proper conversion on due notice. Any loss occurring to him from failure to convert, as here, is not from a risk inherent in his investment but rather from unsatisfactory notification procedures. In principle, the minority bondholders could make a similar argument in our case but, as we will demonstrate, it is not likely that this argument would be successful.

> This paragraph is better, but the writer is still assuming a high level of familiarity with the *Van Gemert* case. You cannot assume that a reader has read the cases that you cite. If your readers have read all the cases, why would they need a memorandum? The writer's job is to identify relevant cases (Common Law Argument Guide Step 1), to compare the facts in these cases to your client's case (Common Law Argument Guide Step 2), and to explain the rationale that a court used to decide the cited cases (Common Law Argument Guide Step 4). Only then can you apply that rationale to your client's case and make a legal conclusion about it.

It is worth noting that in *Van Gemert*, the opinion does not mention the implied covenant of good faith and fair dealing to conclude that the expectation of the debenture holders were not met because the notice of redemption given by Boeing was insufficient. However, future cases relied on *Van Gemert* to apply the good faith and fair dealing doctrine. The decision also indicates (without saying it clearly) that the company's actions were disingenuous and therefore intended to harm the debenture holders. It is likely that the element of intention was relevant to the Court's decision. This case is interesting because it provides us with some elements, such as expectancy and intention, that we need to consider in the Urbania case.

One of the leading cases in exit consents and in our analysis, despite the fact that this is a case decided by a Delaware court (applying the state of Delaware law), is *Katz v. Oak Industries Inc.,* 508 A.2d 873 (1986). In this case, the Plaintiff filed an application for preliminary injunction claiming that the exchange offer for its outstanding debt securities was a coercive device and in its specific circumstances, constituted a breach of contract and a threatened wrong to him and other holders of Oak's securities. It is relevant that it involves a preliminary injunction, which is the most probable action the minority bondholders would choose.

About the preliminary injunction standards, *Katz* cites *Shields v. Shields* (498 A2d. 161):

> "The standards that govern the issuance of a preliminary injunction are well developed and require no elaborate restatement. Essentially this remedy will not issue unless the applicant satisfies the Court that there is a reasonable probability that he or she will ultimately prevail at final hearing on the claims asserted; that unless the remedy is afforded to maintain the status quo until a final hearing can be had, applicant will be injured in a way that is not repairable by an award of damages; and that this threat of irreparable injury to applicant outweighs the threat to defendants of injury that might arise from being wrongfully restrained."

Although this does appear to be a relevant case, I am not sure that this particular discussion is specifically relevant to the Urbania case. Does this seem a bit "off point" to you?

Scrutinizing Plaintiff's ultimate success on the merit of his claim, the Court ruled that: (i) the nature of the relationship between a company and the holders of its debt securities is contractual in nature; (ii) this type of arrangement is usually reflected in a substantial set of documents and are thoroughly negotiated by the parties; (iii) the terms of the contract (and not broad concepts such as fairness) define the company's obligation to its bondholders; (iv) if the company's directors decide to maximize the interests of the company's shareholders "at the expense" of others (such as the bondholders), there is no breach of a fiduciary duty; (v) corporate restructurings might involve a greater risk of loss for bondholders but the courts should not have to provide protection against such enhanced risk.

On Plaintiff's claim that the exchange offer was coercive, the Court ruled that a normative judgment has to be attached to the concept in order to evaluate if the act is "inappropriately coercive" or "wrongfully coercive." In this case, the judgment whether such "coercion" is wrongful or not will derive from the law of contracts. And modern contract law has generally recognized an implied covenant to the effect that each party to a contract will act with good faith towards the other with respect to the subject matter of the contract. The Court quotes a treatise (*Corbin on Contracts,*

This is the major point, but it seems secondary because the prior discussion was so detailed.

Kaufman Supp. 1984): "When the court "implies a promise" or holds that "good faith" requires a party not to violate those expectations, it is recognizing that sometimes silence says more than words, and it is understanding its duty to the spirit of the bargain is higher than its duty to the technicalities of the language." In other words, the implied covenant of good faith and fair dealing is only applicable if one of the parties in a contractual relationship is not getting the benefit of the bargain.

The Court in *Katz* also mentions the concept of foreseeability to explain the legal test to be applied to the case. In its opinion, the Court rules that if it is clear that the parties, if they had thought of negotiating the act later complained of as a breach of the implied covenant of good faith and fair dealing, would have agreed to exclude it from the contract, then a court is justified to rule that such act constitutes a breach of the covenant. On the other hand, the foreseeability concept could be used in the exact opposite way, to convey the idea that it should not be manipulated to allow the covenant of good faith and fair dealing to replace foreseeable issues that could (and sometimes should) arise under the terms of the contract negotiated by the parties. That is to say, if the act was foreseeable, it should have been negotiated by the parties and reflected in the contract.

Furthermore, the Court held that Oak's offer did not breach an implied obligation of the good faith and fair dealing principle. The Court held that the exchange offer's success depends upon the ability and willingness of the issuer to extend an offer that will be a financially attractive alternative to holders. This process is hardly the functional equivalent of the unilateral election of redemption and thus cannot be said in any sense to constitute a subversion by Oak of the negotiated provisions dealing with redemption of its debt. Finally, about the preliminary injunction, the Court held that a court of equity will not issue the extraordinary remedy of preliminary injunction where to do so threatens the party sought to be enjoined with irreparable injury that, in the circumstances, seems greater than the injury the plaintiff seeks to avoid. In our case, this is an important argument because it has to do with the balance of harm. Also in *Sharon Steel*, the Court held that "an interpretation that sacrifices a major interest of one of the parties while furthering only a marginal interest of the other should be rejected in favor of an interpretation which sacrifices marginal interests of both parties in order to protect their major concerns." In the

> This quote from the *Sharon Steel* case seems to be important to the Urbania analysis. It is buried in the middle of this paragraph about the *Katz* case. How could you make this discussion more focused on the exact issues in the Urbania case?

Urbania case, it seems clear that even though the minority bondholders would suffer a harm with the deletion of the gross up clause, if the courts find a violation of the good faith and fair dealing, the harm would be much greater on Urbania, because this would mean that the restructuring failed and the country would most likely default on the bonds entirely.

Katz is especially important for the Urbania case and it would probably be persuasive for New York state courts because it explores concepts such as the "coerciveness", the "benefit of the bargain" and "the foreseeability." For this reason, it is likely a leading case in the study of exit amendments.

> But it is applying the contract law of Delaware. The legal reader would want to know whether the law of Delaware and the law of New York are sufficiently similar so that a court would be confident to follow the reasoning of a Delaware court.

We also examined other cases that suggest that the courts are not likely to recognize a breach of the good faith and fair dealing. In *Metropolitan Life Insurance Company v. RJR Nabisco, Inc.*, 716 F.Supp. 1504 (1989), the Court, applying the state of New York law, held that without express covenant between the parties that would restrict the incurrence of new debt, and no perceived direction to that end from covenants that are express, the court would not imply a covenant to prevent the recent leveraged buy-out. Further, the court held that if such a covenant was implied, it would create an indenture term that, while bargained for in other contexts, was not bargained for in the case and was not even within the mutual contemplation of the parties.

> Again, this description of the *Metropolitan Life* case assumes a lot of knowledge on the part of the legal reader. You cannot assume that the reader has read the cases that you cite. What leveraged buy-out? What covenant? What restriction of debt? Why are these facts similar to or different from the Urbania facts?

In the same direction, *Geren v. Quantum Chemical Corporation*, 832 F.Supp. 728 (1993), also applying the state of New York law, decided that there is no implied covenant restricting any action that might subject plaintiff's investment to greater risk of non-payment. In this case, plaintiffs brought action against corporation to recover from decrease in value of bonds caused by corporation's payment of a special dividend to shareholders. According to the decision, plaintiffs were not able to sustain a claim that an interest or principal payment due to them has not been paid, or that any other explicit contractual right has not been honored. Further, the court found that there was nothing about Quantum's bonds that suggested to

> This seems a little better because the writer explains a little more about the facts of this case. However, the legal reader wants the writer to explicitly compare the facts to the Urbania case. The writer does not do that.

investors that the indenture prohibited the issuer from issuing new debt or paying dividends. *Geren* failed to state a claim based on the contention that defendant's actions violated an implied duty of good faith and fair dealing.

All the above mentioned cases are relevant for our analysis but they are about corporations and not a sovereign state. In *CIBC Bank and Trust Company (Cayman) Limited v. Banco Central do Brasil*, 886 F.Supp. 1105 (1995), the Plaintiffs brought action alleging breach of contract of the agreement to restructure Brazil's sovereign debt. It is a relevant case for Urbania because it deals with debt restructuring of a sovereign country, and also because it is a New York court applying New York law. The Court decided that the "implied covenant sought by plaintiff would not merely complement the *1166 express provisions contained in the Agreement, it would change those provisions and significantly alter the rights of the parties. I refuse to make such an extreme leap on the basis of the cited "sources"—to do so would change the substantive rights of the parties and impair the ability of both debtors and creditors to order their relationships through contractual debt agreements." Thus, it is another case where the court avoided applying the good faith and fair dealing principle.

> This case seems to be highly relevant to the Urbania case. Why is it the last case discussed? As a legal reader, I would have wanted to see this sooner—perhaps the first case to be discussed. Also, I might have wanted more than a paragraph of discussion.
>
> How could you have rearranged the organization of this entire legal discussion to respond more closely to the expectations of a legal reader who is interested in the Urbania case?

IV. CONCLUSION

After analyzing the cases applicable to Urbania, we came to the conclusion that the litigation risk for Urbania would be low if the country decides to proceed with the restructuring of its bonds. The courts are not likely to find that Urbania violated an implied obligation of good faith and fair dealing in relation to the exchange offer the country is proposing to its bondholders. The courts would probably avoid implying a substantive right that was not considered by the parties. Further, the courts would most likely consider Urbania's financial situation and that the alternative to the exchange offer would be the country's default. Specifically in the case of a preliminary injunction, the courts would certainly be concerned about equity in its decision and could be persuaded by the Katz case.

B. SAMPLE MEMORANDUM II

Legal Memorandum

To: Partner

From: Associate

Re: Amendments to Bonds Issued by Urbania

Introduction

Our client, the developing country of Urbania, is in financial distress. Since Urbania is not able to repay its bonds, which are due for repayment at the end of this calendar year ("Current Bonds"), it offered the bondholders an Exit Consent Exchange of the Current Bonds ("Current Bonds") for new bonds, with a maturity date ten years from now ("Exit Bonds"). The Exit Bonds will have lower face value but a higher interest rate than the Current Bonds. The institutional investors ("Majority Bondholders") who hold a majority of 78% of all bonds have accepted this Exit Consent Exchange offer. A small portion of bondholders ("Minority Bondholders"), however, refused to participate in this rescheduling. In order to strongly encourage the Minority Bondholders to accept the Exit Consent Exchange offer, Urbania is considering modifying the Current Bonds by asking the Majority Bondholders to approve deleting a tax clause ("Tax Gross-Up Clause"), originally designed to protect the foreign investors from double taxation. This would make the Current Bonds less attractive to the market. The new, Exit Consent Exchange Bonds would contain a Tax Gross-Up Clause.

> This simple statement puts the client's problem into perspective.

> Notice that the writer has named the two different bonds. By consistently using these two names, the author can avoid confusion between the two different sets of bonds.

> Here, the writer gives some legally significant facts: it is important to know what percentage of the bondholders might be willing to go along with the exchange idea.

> This statement helps the reader to understand why the Tax Gross-Up Clause is valuable to the bondholders.

> This is a clear articulation of the solution Urbania is proposing.

Questions Presented

1. Under New York contract law, does Urbania, according to the amendment clause in the Current Bonds, need the consent of all bondholders in order to delete the Tax Gross-Up Clause?

2. Under New York contract law, would Urbania violate any duties of good faith and fair dealing if it deleted the Tax Gross-Up Clause in the Current Bonds with the consent of the Majority Bondholders, against the wishes of the Minority Bondholders?

> The two questions posed here are straightforward and right on target. You will notice as you read through the memo that these two questions provide the overall organization for the memo.

Brief Answers

1. **No.** The court **would most likely** find that Urbania has, according to the amendment clause, the right to delete the Tax Gross-Up Clause if it has the consent of the Majority Bondholders who hold more than 51% of the face value of the bonds.

2. **No.** The court **would most likely** decide that Urbania would not violate any duty of good faith and fair dealing if it deleted the Tax Gross-Up Clause because the Minority Bondholders would still receive their principal benefits of the bond since the face value and interest rate in the Current Bonds would not be changed by the deletion of the Tax Gross-Up Clause.

> The brief answers in this section act as an outline of the writer's argument in the Discussion section of the memo. They serve as a useful preview for the reader. The US legal reader will find this section useful in familiarizing himself with the client's case and the legal issues that will have to be addressed.

Statement of Facts

Urbania sold the Current Bonds in the international markets; it sold a total of USD 7,500,000.00. Each of the Current Bonds has a face value of USD 1,000.00. These bonds governed by New York law (so-called Yankee bonds), are due for repayment at the end of this calendar year and have an interest rate of 4.5%. 78% of these bonds are held by institutional investors ("Majority Bondholders") and 22% by different kinds of individual investors ("Minority Bondholders").

> This is a complete statement of the facts: both the legally significant facts and some helpful background facts. It also includes the logic behind Urbania's proposed bond restructuring. The inclusion of an explicit analysis of Urbania's motivation and reasoning makes it easier for the reader to understand the writer's reasons for his legal analysis. The Statement of Facts gives the relevant facts of the case, but it also prepares the reader to understand the legal analysis.

Urbania is currently in financial distress and is not able to repay the Current Bonds under the above mentioned conditions. The Urbanese Ministry of Finance therefore met representatives of the Majority Bondholders in order to seek a consensual restructuring of the bonds. Urbania offered to exchange the Current Bonds in an Exit Consent Exchange with new bonds which will mature in ten years ("Exit Bonds"). The Exit Bonds will have a face value of USD 475.00 each at an interest rate of 6%. The Majority Bondholders accepted this offer because it is more likely that Urbania will be able to repay the money ten years from now than it will be at the end of this calendar year. The Minority Bondholders might, however, refuse the exchange offer.

> This paragraph summarizes the situation that Urbania finds itself in—that it is not in a position to repay the bonds and is seeking to restructure the debt in order to avoid defaulting. A minority of the current bondholders might refuse to accept the restructuring plan.

The Majority Bondholders want to have as many bondholders as possible to go along with the deal. This is also the intention of Urbania. Urbania and the Majority Bondholders, therefore, want to amend the Current Bonds with an intention of making them so unattractive that the Minority Bondholders will agree to exchange their Current bonds for the Exit Bonds. According to the amendment clause of the Current Bonds, Urbania has the right to modify the terms and provisions on the Current Bonds if the holders of 51% or more of the principal amount of the bonds agree with it. However, the consent of all bondholders would be required if the modification affected the face value or the interest rate on the bonds.

> These two sentences articulate the motivation for deleting the Tax Gross-Up clause.

> These sentences address the precise language of the modification clause, thus articulating the conditions under which Urbania is allowed to modify parts of the Current Bonds.
>
> It might have been helpful to insert the actual language of the bonds relevant clauses here.
>
> Wouldn't you want to see the language here?

In order to convince the Minority Bondholders to accept the exchange offer, Urbania and the Majority Bondholders intend to delete the so-called Tax Gross-Up Clause from the Current Bonds. All investors have to pay tax in Urbania on the interest they receive for their bonds. Most of the bondholders are not from Urbania, and thus they may be obliged to pay tax in their home countries as well. In order to avoid double taxation, some investors receive, as compensation, a tax credit from their own countries, if the foreign tax is qualified as income tax. Investors who do not have the benefit of such a tax credit from their own countries, have, based on the Tax Gross-Up Clause, the right to get the tax amount back from Urbania.

> This is a clear explanation of how the Tax Gross-Up clause works. This writer knows that the audience for the memorandum might be larger than just the partner who assigned him the task of writing the memo. Other partners in the firm might read the memo. Although partners are smart, they may not all be completely aware of this exit amendment technique. Including this more complete explanation will make all readers' jobs easier and also establish the credibility of the writer.

Urbania and the Majority Bondholders assume that the deletion of this tax gross-up clause would make the Current Bonds less attractive to the market and therefore convince the Minority Bondholders to exchange their Current Bonds for the Exit Bonds, which will have a full tax gross-up clause.

> This paragraph completes the explanation of Urbania's logic in deleting the Tax Gross-Up clause.

Discussion

A Urbania would not be immune from the Laws of the United States

This heading offers a clear, succinct overview of the issue that will be discussed in this section. This helps set appropriate expectations for the reader. Headings like this are common in US Legal English.

Before we start to examine whether Urbania would breach the amendment clause or the rule of good faith and fair dealing if it deleted the Tax Gross-Up Clause, we first need to address the questions whether the sovereign state of Urbania is immune from jurisdiction of the United States courts.

This is a clear statement of the topic of this section of the Discussion.

The Foreign Sovereign Immunities Act of 1976 (FSIA), 28 U.S.C.A. § 1602 et seq., This is a clear statement of the topic of this section of the Discussion. It determines whether a court in the United States of America has jurisdiction over a foreign state. Under this act, a foreign state is immune from the jurisdiction of a court in the United States unless one of the defined exceptions applies. According to the exception in § 1605(a)(2), a foreign state is, under certain circumstances, not immune for an action which "is based upon a commercial activity [. . .]." "Commercial activity" is defined in the FSIA as "either a regular course of commercial conduct or The author notes the appropriate statute that addresses the issue of jurisdiction when a foreign state is involved in the legal proceedings.a particular commercial transaction or act. The commercial character of an activity shall be determined by reference to the nature of the course of conduct or particular transaction or act, rather than reference to its purpose." § 1603 (d).

The author notes the appropriate statute that addresses the issue of jurisdiction when a foreign state is involved in the legal proceedings.

First, the writer points out the relevant statutory law, explaining how it relates specifically to the Urbania case.

The question of immunity for a sovereign country that issued bonds was subject in *Republic of Argentina and Banco Central v. Weltover, Inc.* 504 U.S. 607 (1992). In this case, the sovereign country Argentina issued bonds in the international market in order to refinance its debts. When the bonds began to mature, Argentina unilaterally rescheduled the maturity date of the bonds. The bondholders did not agree with this rescheduling and sued Argentina for payment of the bonds at the United States District Court for Southern District of New York. Argentina claimed that it was immune from the jurisdiction of this court. The

Following common law thinking, the writer does not simply rely on the statute for his argument. He is careful to bolster his argument with appropriate case law. This is the beginning of his first common law argument.

In the preceding sentences, the writer provides the basic facts of the case. This helps the US legal reader to understand how the case fits into the analysis of the Urbania problem.

Supreme Court of the United States held that Argentina's issuance of the bonds was a "commercial activity" under FSIA and that the U.S. court therefore could exercise jurisdiction over the breach of contract claim. Id. 614 et seq. The facts in our case are very similar to the facts in *Republic of Argentina v. Weltover.* Urbania is, analogous to Argentina, a sovereign country that issued bonds in the international market and wants to reschedule the structure of the bonds in order to finance its debts. Therefore, it is **reasonable to conclude** that Urbania's issuance of bonds is also a commercial activity under § 1605 (a) (2) FSIA and that Urbania would, as a consequence, not be protected by immunity. Thus, the courts in the United States **would likely** exercise jurisdiction over Urbania in this matter.

> Here the writer tells us both the court's ruling and its rationale: that Argentina is subject to US courts in this case because it involves commercial activity.

> Here, the writer explicitly compares the facts of the Argentinian case to the Urbania case.

> Here, the writer makes a prediction about how the courts are likely to rule on the issue.
>
> Note the bolded language. Here the author is using appropriate hedging. He cannot know for sure how the court will rule, but he has strong evidence to back his conclusion.

The issue of applicable law was addressed in *Alfred Dunhill of London, Inc. v. Republic of Cuba et al.* 425 U.S. 682 (1976) where the court ruled that the same law needs to be applied to commercial activities of foreign states as to private citizens. In this case, the Cuban Government confiscated the business and assets of the five leading manufacturers of Havana cigars. The Republic of Cuba continued to sell cigars to foreign importers, some of whom were from the United States of America. The former owners of the business sued the U.S. importers for trademark infringement and claimed the purchase price for any cigars that had been shipped to them. The Republic of Cuba was allowed to intervene in the law suit. The Cuban government, claiming it was a sovereign nation immune from such suits, refused to repay money that it had received for shipments subsequent to the intervention. The Supreme Court held that this was a repudiation of a commercial debt which is to be considered as a purely commercial activity and not as an act of state. The court therefore found that the sovereign country Republic of Cuba was also subject to the same law that applies to private parties. Id. 696 et seq., 706. Urbania is, as the Republic of Cuba, a sovereign state. Based on *Republic of Argentina v. Weltover*, Urbania's

> The author is bolstering the argument with another case. The core issue is jurisdiction when a sovereign nation is engaged in commerce. These sentences transition from the analysis one case to another.

> The author summarizes the case's facts. Again, note that the author does not assume that readers will be familiar with this case. The partner may need this information to understand how this case applies to the Urbania case. The writer's job is to explain the law, so readers do not need to do their own legal research.

> Here, the writer provides the court's ruling and rationale.

> In these two sentences, the author clearly links the Cuban case to the Urbania case.

issuance of bonds is considered to be a commercial activity. Thus, a court **would, according to *Dunhill v. Republic of Cuba,* most likely find** that the same law applies for the sovereign country Urbania as for private citizens.

> The author is predicting how the court will rule. Note the bolded language, where the author uses two tactics for nuancing his prediction: the modal "would" plus the phrase "most likely." He also clarifies that the outcome is contingent on the court following the rationale of *Dunhill v. Republic of Cuba.*

To summarize, we have no grounds to believe that Urbania is immune from the courts in the United States of America. Precedent should lead us to assume that the same law applies to it as to private citizens.

> The author offers a final summary of his argument. Such a summary may seem transparent, obvious or redundant, but this is a preferred style in U.S. Legal English.

B It would be in accordance with the amendment clause in the Current Bonds if Urbania deleted the Tax Gross-Up clause

> Again, the subject heading is an important Roadmap for the reader.

According to the Modification Clause in the Current Bonds,

> "[t]he Republic of Urbania may modify any of the terms or provisions contained in the Bonds in any way with the written consent of the holders of not less than 51% in principal amount of the Bonds at the time outstanding, *provided that* (1) if any such modification would change the terms or currency of payment of the principal amount or interest on any Bonds or the amounts thereof, the consent of the holders of all of the Bonds affected thereby is required [. . .]."

> At first glance, this may look like a rather long quote. However, the case hinges on the court's interpretation of this clause. Therefore, it is important to provide the exact language in the memo. It might also be useful to put the full text of the relevant bond clauses in a footnote here so that the reader can refer to them.

Urbania intends to delete the tax gross-up clause with the consent of the Majority Bondholders that hold 78 % of the principal amount of the bonds. Urbania believes that this deletion is in accordance with the above cited amendment clause since more than 51 % of the bondholders agree with it. In contrast, the Minority Bondholders **could** allege that a deletion of the tax gross-up clause would require the consent of all bondholders. They **could** argue that it is the purpose of this modification clause to protect the bondholders' monetary benefit of the investment and that, **if** the Majority Bondholders deleted the tax gross-up clause, the Minority Bondholders **would** end up with less profit. *According to the*

> In the first two sentences of this paragraph, the author lays out Urbania's basic strategy and the logic behind it.

> Starting with the signal 'in contrast,' the writer lays out the probable counterargument to Urbania's strategy. Notice that he provides a thoughtful, respectful version of the counterargument. The underlined sentence provides the reader with a strong statement of the opposition's probable argument. This paragraph explains the essential part of the bond that is likely to be at issue and the two competing interpretations of the modification clause.

Minority Bondholders' interpretation, an amendment that deleted the tax gross up clause would therefore be a breach of contract if only 78% of the bondholders agreed with it. The following paragraphs will discuss how the court would most likely interpret the amendment clause of the Current Bonds and, as a result, whether Urbania would breach this clause if it deleted the tax gross-up provision with the consent of only the Majority Bondholders.

> This entire sentence acts as a transition between the introduction of the two sides of the debate and the writer's predictions.

Under general New York contract law, it is "the fundamental, neutral precept of contract interpretation [. . .] that agreements are construed in accord with the parties' intent. [. . .] 'The best evidence of what parties to a written agreement intend is what they say in their writing [. . .].' Thus, a written agreement that is complete, clear and unambiguous on its face must be enforced according to the plain meaning of its terms." *Ronnie Greenfield et. Al. v. Phillies Records, Inc. et. Al.,* 98 N.Y.2d 562, 569 (New York 2002). In *Sharon Steel Corporation v. Chase Manhattan Bank et. Al.,* 691 F. 2d 1039 (2d Cir. 1982) the United States Court of Appeal interpreted a successor obligator clause in bonds. In dispute was whether a company that sold its assets assigned all liabilities, including the indentures, to the buyer. The court held that the successor obligator clause was not applicable and, consequently, that the indentures and the debentures were due and payable. This case is particularly important to the Urbania case as it is New York case law and addresses the interpretation of a provision in a bond. The case is therefore relevant for the interpretation of the amendment clause in Urbania's Current Bonds and would be very persuasive for the New York State Court even though it does not have a binding force since it was a federal case.

> The writer uses short quotes from *Greenfield v. Phillies Record* to establish the NY court's position on interpreting the intent of parties in a contract: intention is best determined by the language of the contract.

> The author gives some of the facts of the case, but it is not entirely clear how they will apply to *Urbania.* Although both cases have to do with interpreting the language of bonds, the facts and precise issues differ. Sometimes, lawyers must find ways to use cases whose facts do match their client's case. The following paragraphs will explain further what the writer intends to argue about the *Urbania* case.

> This section offers two reasons for the case's importance: it bears on how to interpret a bond's language and it addresses the issue of jurisdiction. The author notes that the case should be persuasive because it was decided in the 2nd Circuit (but is not binding because it wasn't a NY case).

The court found in *Sharon Steel v. Chase Manhattan Bank* that indenture provisions were to be interpreted according to the rule of basic contract law and that the first stage of interpretation was the language of the clause. *Sharon Steel* at 1049; *Ronnie Greenfield* at 569. Regarding the language of the modification clause in the Current Bonds, the consent of all bondholders is required if "a modification would change the terms or currency of payment of the principal amount or interest on any Bond or the amount thereof [. . .]." This restriction clearly protects the "terms or currency of payment of the [invested] principal amount" which Urbania has to pay back. In addition, this part of the amendment clause protects the "interest", in other words the interest rate (in the Current Bonds: 4.5%). It also protects the "amount thereof," which means the effective payment for the interest that results from the calculation of the interest rate on the invested money (in the Current Bond 4.5% x USD 1.000 = USD 45 per Bond each year). Taxes, but also levies, imposts, deductions, charges, etc., are not part of the principal amount, the interest rate or the interest that accrues on the bonds the principal thereof. According to the language of the clause, taxes *etc.* are therefore not in the protected focus of the part of the amendment clause which requires the consent of all bondholders. It might be true that some of the bondholders would *de facto* have less profit without the benefit of the tax gross-up clause. However, neither the "principal amount" nor the "interest" nor the "amount thereof" in the Current Bond would be changed if the tax gross-up clause were deleted. Thus, it is **reasonable** to conclude that it would be in accordance with the language of the amendment clause if Urbania deleted the tax gross-up clause with the consent of the Majority Bondholders.

> This is an important legal principle which the writer began to discuss in the previous paragraph. The writer could give more information about the facts of *Sharon Steel* and the court's reasoning to clarify the significance of that case. Common law reasoning requires the writer to be explicit about how the legally significant facts of his client's case compare to the legally significant facts of a precedent cited.

> This is the language that will be at issue. "Amount thereof" should be understood as the amount of money accumulated from the interest on the bond. This is a logical argument. The author is trying to tie his case to the principle of strict interpretation found in *Greenfield* and *Sharon Steel*. However, it is not clear that all reasonable people would interpret the language this way. That's why this disagreement has risen to a point where a judge must decide how this language should be interpreted. Sometimes lawyers must use logical arguments—especially when there is no case law directly on point. Notice how the writer supports his arguments in the following paragraphs.

> Here the writer is asserting that taxes and other charges are different from the amount of money accumulated through interest.

> Here the writer argues that the language of the bond only protects the principal, the interest rate, and the interest accumulated on the principal; nothing in the language of the bond promises protection from taxes or fees.

> Note the author's use of 'reasonable' here. He is telling the reader that this is a highly probable conclusion, but not the only possible one.

If the court found that the literal reading of the words was not helpful for the interpretation of the amendment clause, it would, according to *Sharon Steel Corporation v. Chase Manhattan Bank,* turn to the underlying purpose of the clause that has to be served. Id. 1049. The purpose of the modification clause in the Current Bonds is to assure effective restructuring of the bonds. This is important for long-term debts, such as the Current Bonds, in order to assure their continuance. An effective restructuring would in most cases not be practicable if it required the consent of all bondholders. The unanimous consent is only justified in order to protect the major clauses of the Current Bonds concerning face amount and interest. A consequence of the Minority Bondholders' interpretation would be that the consent of 100% would be required for each amendment of a term which results in additional expenses for some bondholders. This would make a rescheduling of a bond structure almost impossible. A court would therefore, based on the underlying purpose of the amendment clause, **most probably** find that the consent of more than 51% of all bondholders would be enough in order to delete the tax gross-up clause.

> The author is acknowledging that the principle of literal interpretation may not be enough and is beginning another piece of common law argumentation, again drawing on the *Sharon Steel* case.

> The author is laying out an argument focusing on any reasonable party's purpose for a modification clause, *i.e.* to allow restructuring should the need arise. This is a strong point. Why would the bonds include a modification clause if no one anticipated a possible need for modification? The author further notes that requiring 100% shareholder agreement on all modifications is impractical. However, bond holders are entitled to receive the principal and agreed upon interest rate. These specific elements of the bond are protected by requiring unanimous agreement of the bondholders.

Finally, the court held in *Sharon Steel Corporation v. Chase Manhattan Bank* that, where "contractual language seems designed to protect the interests of *both* parties and where conflicting interpretations [were] argued, the contract should be construed to sacrifice the principal interest of each party as little as possible. An interpretation which sacrifices a major interest of one of the parties while furthering only a marginal interest of the other should be rejected in favor of an interpretation which sacrifices marginal interests of both parties in order to protect their major concerns." Id. 1051. The modification clause in the Current Bonds is designed to protect the interest of all bondholders and addresses therefore both parties. It is difficult to say which party's interests would be sacrificed more if Urbania deleted the Tax Gross-Up clause. On one hand, some of the Minority Bondholders would earn less money

> The author is providing another piece of the court's reasoning in the *Sharon Steel* case. Note that he quotes fewer than two sentences. The court lays out a principle of weighing the interests of both parties.

> The author is applying the court's reasoning directly to the Urbania case.

> The author acknowledges that both parties face potential loss. His contextually effective use of "on one hand' and "on the other hand' here gives the reader the impression that both sides of the case are being seriously considered and weighed. Interestingly, this ties into an important metaphor in the US legal system that concerns balancing factors and the scales of justice.

without the Tax Gross-Up clause. On the other hand, the deletion of the Tax Gross-Up clause is part of Urbania's financial restructuring which is very important for our client and for the Majority Bondholders. If Urbania does not restructure its debt it is likely to default on the bonds entirely Urbania and the Majority Bondholders want to force as many bondholders as possible to accept the Exit Content Exchange offer; an action that is necessary to minimize the risk of Urbania becoming insolvent. Insolvency of Urbania would result in a loss for all the bondholders' invested funds, including the Minority Bondholders' money. Thus, if Urbania is not able to restructure its debt not only Urbania but also all investors would be harmed . For these reasons, a court **would likely consider** the steps to be taken under the Exit Consent Exchange in order to avoid Urbania's bankruptcy more important than the fact that some Minority Bondholders would no longer receive the financial benefit from the Tax Gross-Up clause anymore.

> In these sentences the author has skillfully developed an argument which bolsters Urbania's case. The argument focuses on the possible damage to all parties if Urbania were to default on the debt, thus drawing on the reasoning articulated in the *Sharon Steel* case.

> The author finishes the argument by making a prediction about the probable persuasiveness of this argument with the court.

To sum up, a court **would most likely** find that, according to the modification clause, the Majority Bondholders, who hold more than 51% of the face value of all bonds, have the right to delete the Tax Gross-Up clause.

> The author more forcefully summarizes his predictions. This is a useful conclusion after an important sub-argument in the memo. This helps the reader as he continues to the next part of the memo.

C Urbania would not breach the duty of good faith and fair dealing if it deleted the Tax Gross-Up clause

> Again, notice that the writer uses an effective heading, which alerts the reader to the focus of the following section.

In order to examine whether Urbania would breach the duties of good faith and fair dealing under New York law if it deleted the Tax Gross-Up clause, we first need to establish the NY case law concerning the duties of good faith and fair dealing by looking at some cases of the Court of Appeals of New York.

> The writer here provides a very helpful introduction which alerts the reader that the writer will focus on examining cases from the NY court of appeals. It is very useful to begin each section of the memo with an introduction for the reader.

In New York there is an implied covenant of good faith and fair dealing in the course of contract performance. *Peter Dalton v. Educational Testing Service*, 87 N.Y.2d 384, 389 (New York 1995); *Van Valkenbourgh Nooger & Neville v. Hayden Publishing Company, Inc. et Al.*, 30 N.Y.2d 34, 45 (New York 1972); *Robert L. Rowe v. Great Atlantic & Pacific Tea Company, Inc., et. Al.*, 46 N.Y.2d 62, 67 (New York 1978). "Encompassed within the implied obligation of each promisor to exercise good faith are 'any promises which a reasonable person in the position of the promise would be justified in understanding were included." *Dalton v. Educational Testing Service*, Id. 389; *Rowe v. Great Atl. & Pac. Tea Co.*, Id. 69. In other words, the court has held that precise contractual obligations are not always set out, but the court will follow the reasonable person standard in interpreting unarticulated obligations. "This embraces a pledge that 'neither party shall do anything which will have the effect of destroying or injuring the right of the other party to receive the fruits of the contract." *Dalton v. Educational Testing Service*, Id. 389, with reference to *Kirke La Shelle Co. v. Armstrong Co.*, 263 N.Y. 79, 87 (New York 1933). However, the duty of good faith and fair dealing is limited in a way that the implied obligation has to be consistent with the other provisions of the agreement. *Dalton v. Educational Testing Service* at 389. The facts of these cases will be briefly summarized in the following paragraphs.

In this paragraph, the writer sets out three arguments concerning the concept of good faith and fair dealing in NY contract law: 1) obligations that any reasonable person would assume, even those not explicitly articulated, are considered part of a contract's obligation; 2) GFFD forbids actions that would result in the other party losing the rightful proceeds from the activity regulated by the contract; 3) implicit obligations are limited. At the very least, they cannot contradict expressed contractual provisions. This paragraph provides an overview of previous court rulings, but it isn't a fully formed common law argument. At this point, the writer has only made several generalizations and picked out quotes from cases that seem to uphold the generalizations. If the writer failed to develop the argument further, it would not be very persuasive. This is, however, a useful introduction to the following argument.

In *Dalton v. Educational Testing Service*, a student sued a testing service company which cancelled a test score of the student's Scholastic Aptitude Test ("SAT") because they thought that the first and second tests were completed by separate individuals. Id Despite the fact that the registration bulletin explicitly afforded the student the option to provide the test service with relevant information, the service did not consider the furnished material before it reached the final decision. Id. The court found that the test service "failed to comply in good faith with its own test security procedure." Id. at 393. The student "is

The writer provides the basic facts, rulings and rational of the court in *Dalton v. ETS*. In this case, the court found that ETS violated good faith and fair dealing because it violated its own published procedures when it ignored evidence supplied by the plaintiff, even though its own registration materials, which acted as a contract here, stated that any test taker had the right to submit such materials.

entitled to specific performance of the contract" and thus to "good faith consideration of the material that he sent to the service." Id. at 394.

Similarly, there is also an explicit clause of a contract affected in *Van Valkenbourgh Nooger & Neville v. Hayden Publishing Company.* In this case, an author of books sued his publisher. Id. at 46. The publisher had the contractual duty to publish electronics books, written by the author, and to make its "best efforts" in promotion of these books. Id. 43. The publisher then hired three other writers to prepare a new group of very similar (electronics) books, and he began to advertise them and simultaneously suspended the author's editions. The Court of Appeals found that the publisher did not breach the duty implicit in the contract to act in good faith and therefore denied the order to impose a permanent injunction. However, the court held that the publisher had narrowly breached its contractual undertaking "to use its 'best efforts' in promoting the author's books" and accordingly had to pay compensation for the money damages. Id. at 46.

> Again the writer provides basic facts, rulings and reasoning of the court on a case involving GFFD. Here the author informs us that the court found that a publisher failed to fulfill the explicit agreement to make its best effort to promote an author's books when it stopped publishing and promoting the author's books and simultaneously began publishing and promoting books on a similar topic by other authors.

Finally, in *Rowe v. Great Atlantic & Pacific Tea Company,* a landowner ("lessor") leased a property to a lessee for a "general merchandise business". Id. at 66. The lease agreement contained no restriction on assignment of the lease to a third party. The lessee shut down its operations and assigned the lease to a third party which operated a chain of supermarkets. The lessor sued the lessee to recover possession and money damages, claiming that this assignment was a breach of the implied duty of good faith and fair dealing because the lessee had sublet the property without express permission from the lessor. The Court of Appeals held that the lessee did not act in bad faith. It found that the existence of an implied covenant "is to be recognized only if it is clear that a reasonable landlord would not have entered into the lease without such an understanding, for it is only in such a situation that it can be said with the requisite certainty that to refuse to recognize such covenant would be to deprive the landlord of the fruits of his bargain." Id. at 70. In other words, the court held that since

> In parallel to the argumentation in the previous two paragraphs, the writer provides the facts, ruling and reasoning of the court in a pertinent case. In this particular case, the court ruled that the defendant did not violate the doctrine of GFFD. The key points in the reasoning were that 1) no language in the contract specifically prevent the lessee from subletting the property in question and any reasonable landlord who did not want such a sublease would include restrictive language in the contract; and 2) since the lessor continued to receive the agreed upon rent, he was not deprived of the bargained for fruits of the contract.

nothing was expressly written in the contract that forbad the lessee from subletting the property and because the lessor continued to receive the agreed upon rent, the lessor had not been deprived of the fruits of the bargain. Any reasonable landlord who would not allow such a sublet would put such a restriction in the contract.

According to the New York case law set out above, a court **would most likely** find that Urbania would not breach the covenant of good faith and fair dealing if it deleted the tax gross-up clause in order to force the Minority Bondholders to accept the offered Exit Consent Exchange. Considering the cases, we can conclude that the court is reluctant to decide a breach of an implied duty of good faith and fair dealing (see *Van Valkenbourgh Nooger & Neville v. Hayden Publishing Company and Rowe v. Great Atlantic & Pacific Tea Company.*). The court found a breach of good faith and fair dealing only in the *Dalton v. Educational Testing Service* case, where the testing service failed to comply with an explicit provision of its own test security provision. In *Van Valkenbourgh Nooger v. Hayden,* there was also an explicit clause that was affected by a party of the contract. The court denied a general breach of good faith and fair dealing; however, it found that the contractual duty was narrowly breached. Urbania's action is in accordance with all explicit provisions in the Current Bonds. As explained in section B above, nothing in the explicit language of the modification clause excludes Urbania from changing (or deleting) the Tax Gross-Up clause, as long as the holders of more than 51% in principal amount of the Current Bonds agree with the action.

> In the following paragraphs, the writer develops his predictions concerning how the court is likely to find in the Urbania case, given previous NY case law.

> The author offers a general conclusion about the court's reluctance to find a breach of GFFD if the duty is an **implied** one.

> Here the writer compares the basic facts of the Urbania case with those of the three NY cases. He is continuing to deal with the notion of breach of the explicit language of the contract. He notes that the language of the Urbania bond allows for amendments to the bond with 51% agreement. The tax gross-up clause is not one of the provisions of the bond explicitly protected by unanimous consent.

Another question is whether Urbania would affect the Minority Bondholders' negotiated fruits of the Current Bonds if it deleted the Tax Gross-Up clause. *See Dalton v. Educational Testing Service,* at 389. Even though some bondholders would in fact make less profit without the benefit of the Tax Gross-Up clause, they would still receive their principal "fruits of the contract" since the principal amount and the interest on the Bonds would not be changed (see interpretation in section B).

> The author makes the argument that the principal fruits of the contract are payment of the principal plus the agreed upon interest. Deletion of the tax gross up clause would not change the bondholders' receipt of either of those specific amounts.

Since there is no breach of good faith and fair dealing in regard to an explicit provision, it is important to examine whether a reasonable bondholder would only enter into the contract with the understanding of a duty of good faith and fair dealing that prohibits the deletion of the Tax Gross-Up clause unless 100% of the bondholders agree to the change. *See Rowe v. Great Atlantic*, at 70. It is Urbania's aim to restructure its debts in order to avoid default on its obligations under the Current Bonds. The offered Exit Consent Exchange of the Current Bonds for the Exit Bonds will most probably allow Urbania to perform its bond obligations. This exchange is very important for the Majority Bondholders, because this may be the best way for them to receive at least a part of the expected return on their investment. Urbania and the Majority Bondholders therefore intend to encourage as many bondholders as possible to accept the exchange offer. They hope to reach this aim by deleting the Tax Gross-Up clause. Such restructurings are common and sometimes necessary to avoid insolvency of the bond issuer. The bondholders would appear to be aware of this, as witnessed by the negotiated language that protects the principal, interest rate and due date by requiring unanimous consent in order to change any of these features of the bond. At the time parties enter into a bond contract, it is not foreseeable whether a potential future restructuring will be considered. The bondholders would therefore not contractually exclude the opportunity to amend the structure of a bond in ways not covered by the modification clause, such as by deleting the Tax Gross-Up clause. Thus, the court **would most likely** come to the conclusion that a reasonable holder of the Current Bonds would not be justified in understanding that the prohibition to delete the Tax Gross-Up clause in order to reschedule Urbania's financial structure was included in the implied obligation of good faith and fair dealing. For these reasons, the holdings in the above mentioned cases of the Court of Appeal of New York **should be** persuasive arguments against a claim of a breach of an implied rule of

Here the author provides a transition between the arguments dealing with violation of explicit language and violation of implicit duties. Recall that he established earlier, in reference to the *Rowe* case, that the reasonable person standard is used in determining implicit duties.

This is a thoughtfully articulated argument, laying out the positive reasons motivating Urbania's restructuring proposal.

This is an important, common sense argument, which fits with the reasonable person standard. If restructurings are common, a reasonable investor would not expect an implied covenant that changes to the bond in ways that are not explicitly protected in the modification clause. These modifications of the basic "fruits of the contract" can only occur with unanimous agreement of the bondholders.

These two sentences offer logical expansion of the common sense argument.

The author concludes that the court is likely to determine that a reasonable bond holder would not, at the time the bond was issued, interpret the Tax Gross-Up clause as part of the bond protected by unanimous consent.

Here the writer ties the common sense argument to previous case law, thus making it part of a common law argument. Explicitly tying the common sense argumentation back into legal precedent, strengthens the argument considerably.

good faith and fair dealing and are therefore in favor of our client Urbania.

However, the Minority Bondholders could raise the issue that these cases would not be relevant for Urbania's action since the facts are too different. The United States District Court, S.D. New York, denied a breach of good faith and fair dealing under New York law in the following two cases where the facts are very similar to the ones of in the Urbania case.

> This paragraph begins to offer a counter-argument that the opposition might make. The writer points out that there are at least two district court cases decided in NY whose facts are closer to those of the Urbania case and in which the court held that the doctrine of GFFD was not violated.

In the first case, *Metropolitan Life Insurance Company v. RJR Nabisco, Inc.*, 716 F.Supp. 1504 (S.D. New York 1989), bondholders had sued the corporation that issued the bonds in order to recover a multimillion dollar loss of value of the bonds that resulted from a leveraged buy-out. The bondholders claimed that the actions in connection with the leveraged buy-out drastically decreased the value of the bonds by "misappropriating the value of those bonds to help finance the [leveraged buy-out] and to distribute an enormous windfall to the company's shareholders" Id. at 1506. The court held that in contracts, like bond indentures, an implied rule such as good faith and fair dealing must be derived from the language in the bond and cannot give the bondholders rights that are not in accordance with the terms. Id. at 1517. It also found that the leveraged buy-out did not violate any implied covenants in the bond indenture which should ensure that the parties act in accordance with the "bargained-for rights." Id. at 1519. But, the court does not permit "an implied covenant to shoehorn into an indenture additional terms" (Id.) and is properly "reluctant to imply into an integrated agreement terms that have been and remain subject to specific, explicit provisions, where the parties are sophisticated investors, well versed in the market's assumptions, and do not stand in a fiduciary relationship with one another." Id. at 1522. In order for the court to find a violation of implied duties of GFFD, the company must have "either exhibited bad faith or destroyed [the bondholders] *legitimate*, protected expectations." Id.

> The facts of *Met Life* are more closely aligned to those of the Urbania case because they involve bondholders arguing that certain actions taken by the bond issuer decreased the value of the bond, just as deleting the tax gross up clause would decrease the value of the bonds. This represents a comparison of the facts of the two cases.

> The court ruled that implied duties must derive from the language of the bonds.

> The court has explicitly stated that implied duties cannot be construed in such a way that bondholders are given additional protections that they did not bargain for at the time the contract was issued. In other words, the court has expressed reluctance to grant protections that are not explicitly mentioned in the bond.

The second case, *Preston M. Geren v. Quantum Chemical Corporation,* 832 F. Supp. 728 (S.D. New York 1993), faced an almost identical issue as the above mentioned *Metropolitan Life Insurance v. RJR Nabisco* case. Bondholders sued the corporation which had issued the bonds and sought damages because the corporations' distribution of a special dividend to its common stockholders decreased the value of the bonds by approximately 50%. The bonds had a face amount of USD 1,250,000,000 which declined after the distribution of the dividend by USD 625,000,000. The bondholders claimed that the corporation's action violated an implied duty of good faith and fair dealing by "diminishing and misappropriating [its] assets [. . .] by incurring substantial debt to fund the special dividend." Id. at 731. The United States District Court, S.D. New York held that these allegations failed to state a claim and that "there [was] no implied covenant restricting any action that might subject [bondholders'] investment to greater risk of non-payment. What [bondholders] have failed to allege is that an interest or principal payment due them has not been paid, or that any other explicit contractual right has not been honoured." Id. at 733.

In the *Geren* case, as in the *Met Life* case, the bondholders argued a violation of GFFD because the company undertook actions which resulted in the bonds losing market value.

Using the exact language of the court, the writer demonstrates that the standard for violating the bond is failure to pay the interest or principal. Note that in presenting these two cases, the writer primarily relies on paraphrase and summary, and uses direct quotations from the court judiciously.

The crucial similarity between *Metropolitan Life Insurance v. RJR Nabisco, Geren v. Quantum Chemical* and the Urbania case is the fact that the issuer of the bonds took some financial actions in its favour that caused harm to its bondholders. In *Metropolitan Life Insurance v. RJR Nabisco* the company undertook actions in order to finance a leveraged buy-out that decreased the value of the bonds. Similarly in *Geren v. Quantum Chemical,* the corporation, and accordingly the shareholders, benefited from a huge dividend that decreased the value of the bond. The situation in Urbania is analogous to these cases. Urbania, the issuer of the bonds, intends to delete the tax gross-up clause in order to force the bondholders to exchange their Current Bonds for the Exit Bonds. This action would be an advantage for Urbania since it would help to reschedule its financial structure but it would be a disadvantage for the

The writer forcefully lays out the key similarities between the two legal precedents and the Urbania case.

Here the actions taken by *Met Life* and *Quantum Chemical* are clearly and artfully reiterated to amplify the reasoning presented in the previous sentence.

A clear, straightforward transition to Urbania.

A strong, careful piece of analytical reasoning that shows the underlying parallels between the actions taken by *Met Life* and *Quantum* and those proposed by Urbania.

Minority Bondholders who do not want to accept the exchange offer and, as a result, could not benefit from the Tax Gross-Up clause any more.

According to both *Metropolitan Life Insurance v. RJR Nabisco* and *Geren v. Quantum,* it is a breach of an implied duty of good faith and fair dealing if an interest or principal payment has not been paid or if another explicit contractual clause has not been complied with. As shown above, Urbania would not dishonour an explicit provision of the bond if it deleted the tax gross-up clause (see interpretation in section B, and reasoning in section C). Moreover, the Minority Bondholders would still receive the principal payment and the interest (Interpretation in section B).

> This paragraph provides a clear, succinct summary of the important elements of the author's argument arising from *Met Life* and *Geren*.

Finally, the court is especially reluctant to apply the rule of good faith and fair dealing when the parties are "sophisticated investors" who do not own a fiduciary duty to each other. *Metropolitan Life v. RJR Nabisco,* Id. at 1522. In our case, we do not know who the Minority Bondholders in particular are. Some of them might be professional investors, others might be just individual investors. Most of them might not be as sophisticated as the financial institutions in *Metropolitan Life v. RJR Nabisco*. However, since sovereign bonds, such as the ones issued by Urbania, are uncommon for lay persons, it can at least be assumed that the Minority Bondholders are well versed in the capital market. Furthermore, we can assume that the Minority Bondholders do not have a fiduciary relationship to each other. Thus, a court might be even more reluctant to find a breach of the implied covenant in the Current Bonds of Urbania than it might be in other cases. Hence, upon reviewing these two cases, the court **would most likely** decide in favour of Urbania.

> The author is introducing a new argument, based on the *Met Life* case which involves the notion of sophisticated investors.

> The author concedes that the exact background of the investors is not known. This shows that the writer is trying to be objective in his assessment of the client's case.

> The writer offers a common sense argument that not many people are involved in buying sovereign bonds, therefore the investor in Urbania's bonds probably would be considered sophisticated investors.
>
> This is an inference that the writer makes based on the other cases.

However, the arguments based on the previous cases contain two weaknesses. First, New York state courts would not be bound by these cases because they were held by federal courts. Nevertheless, since the courts in these cases applied New York state law, they would be highly persuasive for a New York state court.

> This sentence serves as a transition to introduce possible counter arguments.

> The writer is careful to present possible weaknesses in his argument. The fact that the two most analogous cases are federal cases and not NY state cases means they are not binding on the NY court.

The second weakness is that there is, compared to our Urbania case, one element in the facts that is not present in the above cited cases. Urbania intends to delete the Tax Gross-Up clause in order to *force* the Minority Bondholders to exchange their Current Bonds for the Exit Bonds. In *Metropolitan Life Insurance Company v. RJR Nabisco* and in *Geren v. Quantum Chemical Corporation,* the bondholders were not forced or encouraged into an action. In contrast, *Moise Katz v. Oak Industries Inc,* 508 A.2d 873 (Del. Ch. 1986) contains a very similar situation as the Urbania case in which the issuer of the bonds wanted to force the bondholders to agree with an exchange offer. The minority or holdout bondholders who did not consent to this exchange offer risked having important contractual protections removed from their bonds through an exit amendment. Id. at 876. The owner of long term debt securities sued the company that issued the securities. He sought "to enjoin the consummation of an exchange offer and consent solicitation made by [the company] to holders of various classes of its long-term debt" and alleged, "that the exchange offer [was] a coersive device and [. . .] constitute[d] a breach of contract" Id. at 875. The Court of Chancery of Delaware decided that coercion was not a term with legal status and there was no breach of implied duties of good faith and fair dealing.

> The author presents another potentially important weakness in the case. None of the prior cases involves the bond issuer undertaking actions with the intent of putting pressure on the bondholders to take a particular action.

> The facts, reasoning and ruling of a Delaware court in the *Katz* case are laid out. The facts are parallel to the Urbania case. The court's ruling and reasoning would seem to favor Urbania.

The weakness of *Katz v. Oak Industries Inc.* is that it was decided under the law of Delaware. Therefore, the case is not binding for New York State Courts. However, **since** the facts of this case and that of the Urbania case are almost identical and since the Court of Chancery of Delaware based its reasoning on *Corbin on Contracts*, which is a very well established treatise in the United States, this case **could be very persuasive** for a New York State.

> The author is careful to point out that although the *Katz* case would seem to support Urbania's case, it is a Delaware case and therefore not binding on a NY court. However, the case is likely to be highly persuasive with a NY court.

Conclusion

The legal risks **would be low** if our client Urbania deleted the Tax Gross-Up clause as part of an Exit Consent Exchange strategy. First, the deletion of the Tax Gross-Up clause would most likely not violate the modification clause in the Current Bonds. Because the deletion would not affect the face value and the interest rate in the Current Bonds, according to the modification clause, the unanimous consent of the bondholders would not be required. Second, Urbania would most probably not be held to breach any duty of good faith and fair dealing if it deleted the Tax Gross-Up clause because the deletion of the Tax Gross-Up clause is not expressly protected by the language of the Current Bonds. Moreover, prior case law indicates that the court will be reluctant to give additional protections to the bondholders that do not clearly arise from the language of the bond. Further, the court has previously held that as long as the bond holder receives the principal and interest due, the fruits of their contract have been preserved.

> Here, the writer gives a clear, but nuanced prediction concerning that it is likely that a court would rule in favor of Urbania.

> Again, the writer gives a clear, succinct summary that answers the two key questions laid out at the beginning of the memorandum.